GETTING TO GO

INDIGORIVER
PUBLISHING

Getting to Go!

Lessons from an Entrepreneur and CPA About Starting a Business from Scratch

DAVID R. PETERS

CPA, CFP®, CLU, CPCU

Getting to Go: Lessons from an Entrepreneur and CPA About Starting a Business from Scratch

Library of Congress Control Number: 2025926932
ISBN: 978-1-969935-18-3 (paperback) 978-1-969935-19-0 (ebook)

Editors: Abigail Dengler, Jorge David Remy
Cover and Interior Design: Emma Elzinga

Printed in the United States of America

First Edition

3 West Garden Street, Ste. 718
Pensacola, FL 32502
www.indigoriverpublishing.com

Ordering Information:

Quantity sales: Special discounts are available on quantity purchases by corporations, associations, and others. For details, contact the publisher at the address above.

Orders by US trade bookstores and wholesalers: Please contact the publisher at the address above.

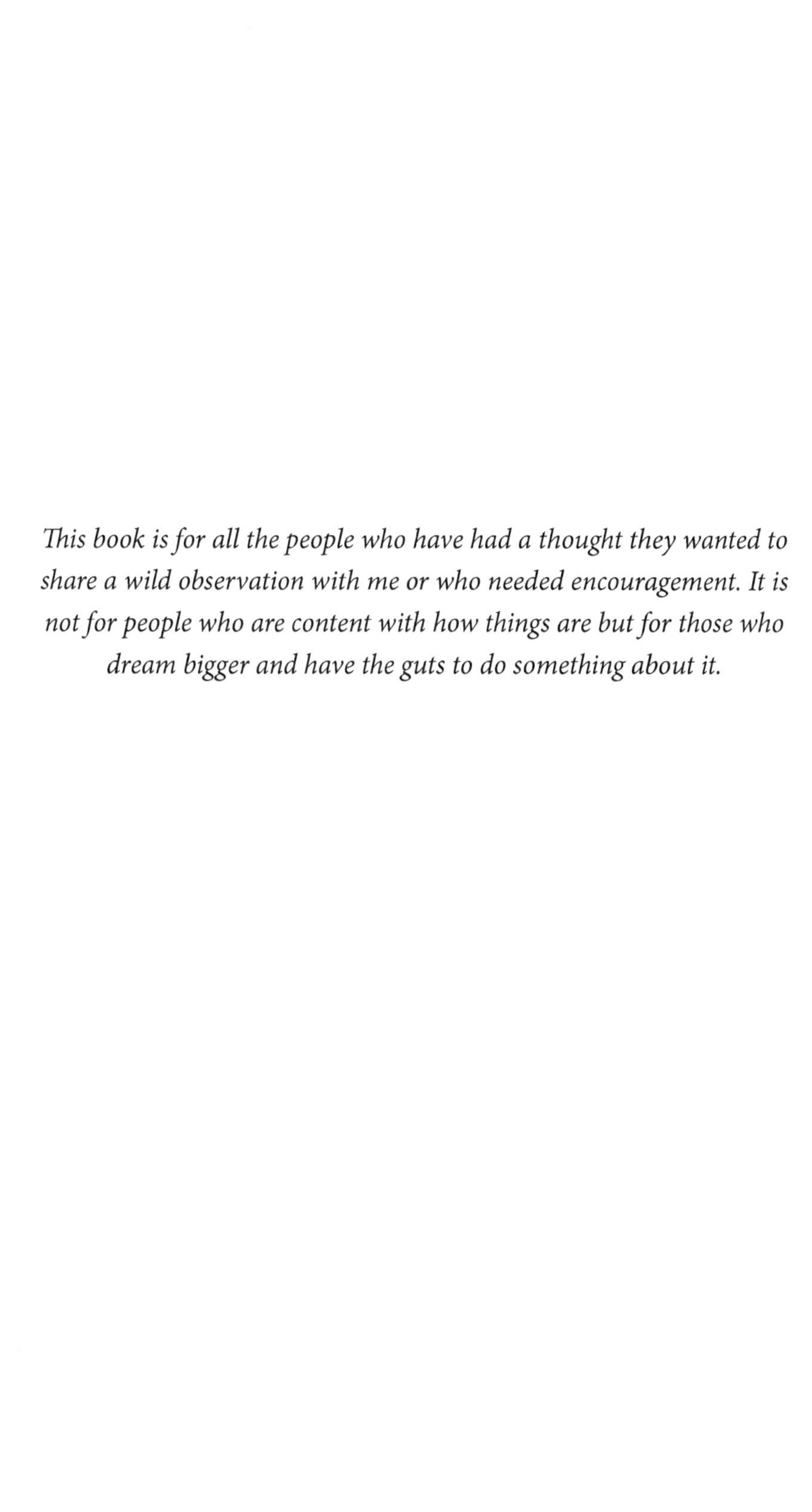

This book is for all the people who have had a thought they wanted to share a wild observation with me or who needed encouragement. It is not for people who are content with how things are but for those who dream bigger and have the guts to do something about it.

CONTENTS

PREFACE

Answers You (Almost) Don't Want to Hear

"But I thought I didn't have to do this. You said I didn't have to do this! I am at the airport getting ready to board a plane. I can't get to this until after Christmas. Do I really have to deal with this now?"

My clients' questions were difficult ones for me to hear. To be fair, I don't think they wanted to hear my answers either. After all, it was December 23rd, and they were trying to escape the hustle and bustle of their growing interior design business for a few days. They had record profits in 2024 and were going away for some much-deserved time off. They didn't want to deal with vendor invoices or last-minute change order requests from clients. They *definitely* did not want to hear from me!

However, as a tax practitioner and financial advisor, my job is to ensure that my clients take care of what they have to, whether they want to or not.

"I know the timing on this is horrible. However, there are significant penalties if you don't register your business with FINCEN. I'm sorry, but you need to do this. I can't do it for you. You have to do it.

However, if you have any questions, I will try my best to answer them or point you to someone who can. Okay?"

After fifteen minutes of telling me how bad my timing was and how little time they had to get away, my clients reluctantly agreed to file their beneficial ownership information report once their airplane landed and they could get to a computer. They weren't happy with me for calling with a "hair on fire" emergency right before Christmas. However, they knew I was trying to keep them out of compliance trouble and help keep their dreams of growing a small business alive.

As I sat there staring at my iPhone right after our phone call ended, I couldn't help but think of how many things small business owners need to know. Aside from trying to build a client base and market their products, they must also be aware of compliance, insurance, accounting, legal, and countless other issues. Not only this, but it is never a one-and-done with small business owners. They need to be constantly aware of ongoing changes related to their business.

Take the Financial Crimes Enforcement Network (FINCEN) beneficial ownership information (BOI) reporting requirements that I called my clients about on that cold December afternoon:

- The Corporate Transparency Act was enacted in 2021. It mandated that nearly every small business owner doing business in the United States was required to file certain information about themselves and their small business sometime before December 31, 2024.
- On December 3, 2024 (right before the deadline), a federal judge in the Texas Top Cop Shop case issued a nationwide injunction prohibiting the enforcement of the BOI requirements anywhere in the country. This was welcome relief for over 30 million small businesses in the United States whose owners

were supposed to comply with this requirement. They didn't have to do anything while the injunction was in place, so they were off the hook for the time being.

- On December 23, 2024, the Court of Appeals issued a stay of the injunction. In other words, small business owners were again required to comply with BOI reporting! This gift of holiday cheer from our court system necessitated many last-minute calls from practitioners (like me) to their clients to ensure they knew about this requirement and the stiff penalties for non-compliance. After all, a business call during the holidays is annoying. However, if it keeps the client from thousands of dollars in potential fines and prison time, that's probably worth it!
- On December 26, 2024, the Fifth Circuit Court of Appeals vacated the stay of the injunction. What does that mean? After three days of worry from small business owners, once again, they were no longer required to file their BOI report with FINCEN.[1]
- On January 23, 2025, the Supreme Court granted the federal government's motion to stay the injunction issued in the Texas Top Cop Shop case. However, companies were still not required to file their BOI report with FINCEN because a second federal judge had issued another nationwide order that prevented BOI reporting!
- On February 19, 2025, FINCEN confirmed that small business owners were again required to submit BOI reporting with new reporting deadlines.

---

1 FINCEN did say during all this back-and-forth that companies could still voluntarily file, even if the various injunctions were still in place.

- Finally, on March 21, 2025, FINCEN said that only foreign companies—not domestic companies—would need to comply with the BOI reporting requirements.

Looking at this list, it is no wonder that small business owners are constantly worried about their business. As a financial professional, I struggled to keep up with the almost daily changes around BOI reporting. I didn't blame my clients for feeling overwhelmed! After all, who wouldn't be? All this back-and-forth is enough to make a small business owner with the strongest stomach feel sick! Even as I write this, the saga of BOI reporting has still not entirely played out. FINCEN is still finalizing the BOI requirements. Practitioners are still trying to navigate the maze of compliance. Small business owners can only hope to see what is coming before it is too late!

In my experience, it is not the requirements that a small business owner knows about that keep them up at night. It is all the things that they don't know. Small business owners don't get worried about the complexities of their industry or the challenges of their idea. They worry about the things outside of their wheelhouse. They think, "What should I know about, but just don't?" And "What would put my business at risk?" Or even "Is there an important change I'm unaware of?" These are their worries. What follows are the answers they (almost) don't want to hear.

INTRODUCTION

Getting to Go: A Lesson from a Paper Company

"Okay. Now what?" I sat at my kitchen table, staring blankly at a half-full cup of coffee and listening to the honking horns of impatient motorists on their way to work. Everyone was so happy for me on Friday. "Wow! That's great that you're going into business for yourself!" "How exciting! I know you'll be successful!" I felt exuberant and energized. I was excited about my future.

Now, it was Monday, and reality had set in. I realized I had no plan! No one was telling me what to do or how to do it. It was just me, my coffee getting cold, and the symphony of angry horns from people going to work outside my condo in the city of Richmond, Virginia.

It is not unusual to feel lost when starting a business. After all, what task is more daunting than that? Everything is on your shoulders, from getting clients and figuring out where to market to purchasing office supplies and the coffee maker. It all just seems so big! In the movies, all you need is a good montage, and suddenly, you are all set up and successful. Real life is a bit different. While going into business for yourself can be financially and professionally rewarding, it typically takes a while to get there. More often, in the beginning, it just feels like . . . well, work! It is slow, thankless, and tiring. In those long and painful beginning days, the only thing that can keep you going is passion. Simply put, if you don't love what you do, you won't make it. When money is tight, days are long, and new jobs are slow to come, passion is all you have. So, how do you figure out if you really love what you do that much?

Getting to Go

When I was in my teens, I attended soccer camp every summer. I was not a natural athlete by any stretch. I was short, somewhat overweight, and I had asthma growing up. To make matters worse, August days in Chicago could be unmercifully hot. However, I loved the sport. I loved the feeling of giving the perfect pass to a teammate waiting by the opposing net. I loved being drenched with sweat and pushing my body to the limit. I loved the satisfying soreness in my legs and feet as I walked off the field, letting me know that I had accomplished something.

This unique duality made me both dread and look forward to soccer camp each year. The challenge was intense, but the game was beautiful. Not to mention that it was a privilege to play. Buying Adidas cleats, Umbro shorts, and Nike number 5 soccer balls costs money. For this reason, I always described soccer camp as something I was "getting to go" to each year. It was an alluring challenge that I was privileged enough to experience. It was something that I wanted to do, even though I knew it would not be easy.

The phrase "getting to go" can mean a few different things. We often describe an event that not everyone has the opportunity to experience as something we are "getting to go" to. When I was asked to present my first academic paper at the Academy of Financial Services conference several years ago, I told everyone who would listen that I was "getting to go" and present my findings to other professionals in Las Vegas. In this way, the phrase "getting to go" implies optimism and privilege. It communicates that the opportunity is exciting but not available to everyone. It is a challenge that you are looking forward to.

However, "getting to go" can also carry the sense of a beginning point—a point at which you can fully start something. One of my first accounting supervisors used to say that you had to talk to the client before you could "get to go." What he meant by this phrase is that you needed to have a conversation with the client about their personal situation before you could begin the billable work of preparing the tax return, putting together financial statements, or even entering the bookkeeping journal entries. Until you understood the context of the work and the client's needs, you couldn't start the job. In this way, the phrase "getting to go" can also involve overcoming obstacles to commence the real work you need and want to do.

Before you go into business for yourself, you must "get to go." You must recognize the challenge in front of you as a privilege that not everyone can experience. You have to reach the point where you are mentally prepared to begin, no longer held back by fear of the unknown.

The decision to start my own business did not happen right away for me. My father had run a successful sheet metal fabrication shop in my hometown of Grayslake, Illinois. I had seen the long days he put in and the worries over how fast customers were paying. Being his own boss looked tough to me, even as a child. As an adult, I also knew that statistically, most startups fail. Logically, it made no sense to start my own business. So why did I do it?

I had to. I had no choice. My desire to discover whether I could grow a successful business outweighed my fear and anxiety. I gave myself permission to let go of my "common sense" and try something new and exciting. I knew from my dad that the challenge would be excruciating, but I didn't care. In short, I had "gotten to go."

I have had the pleasure of working for several good companies. I was lucky enough to have great mentors throughout my career who pushed me in the right ways and encouraged me when I made mistakes. Don Fontana, the owner of the first CPA firm I ever worked for as an intern, pushed me to be a better tax preparer and taught me the analytical skills necessary to be a good CPA. Tim MacAleese and Susan Gaidos, who rejuvenated my career after a terrible experience at a previous job, taught me to learn from my mistakes and always strive to be better. Andrew Rose, who hired me into my first executive role, taught me that if you care about people, you will help them to be their best (which makes you better too).

Many people go into business for themselves because they are so disgusted with their current work situation that they just can't go on another day. On the contrary, my work experience was very positive. I consider myself lucky to have had these people in my life. They taught me invaluable lessons, both personally and professionally.

However, even during these positive and transformative times, something in the back of my mind always wondered: what if? What if I could do this myself? What if I could handle the pressure of leading an organization? What if I could find people who shared the same passion for the work I was doing? I would think these things on my drive to work in the morning and when I put my head on my pillow at night. I would find myself contemplating how much capital I would need, what I would invest in first, and which positions I would need to fill when. I would think about what ads would look like for my services and what customers might be interested in what I did. Over time, those thoughts grew increasingly detailed and planned out. These nagging thoughts kept getting louder with each passing day. My desire to answer these questions became stronger than statistical warnings or red flags.

One day, I simply gave myself permission to find out. I didn't have a formal business plan or Wall Street investors backing me. I just wanted to answer the question that was burning inside of me each day.

It never makes logical sense to go into business for yourself. Most startups fail. Most people can't handle the pressure. There is never enough money or resources. And you will nearly always have family members and close friends telling you that you are crazy. I have had countless people tell me they will go into business for themselves "once they are a little bit more financially secure." I have had countless people tell me they just want to gain "a little more experience" before trying to do it independently. These people have not gotten to go yet. The comfort of their current life still outweighs their desire to take the leap and go into business for themselves. You know you have gotten to go when the determination to take a chance on yourself is so strong that you simply no longer care about all the reasons why you shouldn't.

Here is the reality: There is no such thing as going into business for yourself without taking a risk. Period. If you are waiting for the timing to be perfect, it never will be. You just reach a point where you don't care whether or not you fail. It no longer matters to you if you make less money than in your current job. You just can't stand the "what ifs" in the back of your brain anymore. Once you are there, you are at "go." You give yourself permission. You take a chance. You become brave. And you jump in.

One of my favorite TV shows of all time is the American version of *The Office*. In one episode, the show's main character, Michael Scott, decides to start his own paper company. Pam, a friend and colleague of Michael's, has decided to go work for him. After a terrible first day full of setbacks, Pam is distraught and seemingly regrets her impulsive decision to join Michael in this new venture.

> ***Michael Scott:*** *I want you to listen to me. Because I want to tell you the situation that we are both in right now, 'kay? You quit your job. I quit my job. We both quit. Those are the facts. That's what happened. Now, what are our choices right now? Because you know, kiddo, you quit.*
>
> ***Pam:*** *Yeah.*
>
> ***Michael Scott:*** *So, what are our options? Well, we can start this paper company. We can try. Or . . . that's it. That's our only option. Because we quit. Pam, I do my best work when people don't believe in me. I remember in high school, my math teacher told me I was gonna flunk out. And know what I did? The very next day, I went out and I scored more goals than anyone else in the history of the hockey team. See what I mean? I thrive on this. I thrive on it. So, I'm gonna go inside. I'm going to make some calls, I'm gonna get us an office space, and I'm going to show you why you joined this company. All right?*[2]

Admittedly, Michael's comedic naivete is hysterical. However, this scene illustrates the idea of getting to go well. Michael had mentally moved past all the flaws in his plan to start a new paper company. He didn't care about failure or other options. In his mind, there was no choice. He had reached go. He had allowed himself to move past the doubt and go to work.

Many people have come up to me after seminars or at conferences and expressed a desire to start their own business due to frustration with their current working situation. While each person gets to go in a different way, this is a dangerous line of thinking. If you are just frustrated with your current job, you should find a new one. For every toxic working environment out there, there are several

---

2 *The Office*, season 5, episode 23, "Two Weeks," written by Justin Spitzer, directed by Gene Stupnitsky, aired April 9, 2009, on NBC.

healthy ones. Don't become an entrepreneur out of spite. Become an entrepreneur because you can't shake the feeling that you can do something better. Become an entrepreneur because you see an opportunity and need to find out if you can take advantage of it. Once your desire to answer this calling outweighs anything else, you have gotten to go— and it is time to jump in with both feet.

Hollywood and the Startup Misconception

Whether we realize it or not, Hollywood paints an often unrealistic and glorified picture of a startup business. This façade shapes many of the misconceptions I commonly hear from those considering entrepreneurship. For this reason, we must take a moment to separate fact from fiction so you can understand the reality of what you are considering. By doing this, you will either move closer to go or lose the allure of the startup business. Either way is progress. Let's look at a few misconceptions.

Misconception 1: I will get paid more as the boss.

In most startup businesses, margins tend to be thin. It takes capital to buy equipment, file incorporation papers, and market the product or service. Unless you have acquired an existing business, developing a client base may take some time. While you may make more money in the long run if you are successful, owners more often make very little in the first few years. Simply put, the company doesn't have the money to pay the owner, so you will probably make less initially.

Misconception 2: I can make my own hours as the boss.

This one is both true and false. In many jobs, employees are told when they are supposed to be at work and doing their job. It is true that if you are in charge, no one is necessarily standing over your shoulder telling you when to do what. You do have the flexibility to go to children's sporting events or go out to eat with your spouse or friends. There is no official limit on the number of days off you can take.

However, to say that one works less as their own boss is often incorrect. If no employees are around to help you with a particular task, the responsibility falls on you. If a job needs to get done for a client and no one can help, you are responsible for staying late and finishing it. If no one is in charge of a particular business need, the responsibility becomes yours by default. So, while the actual hours are less rigid, being your own boss often means taking on *more* responsibility, not less. More responsibility often means extended hours and more time involved.

Misconception 3: I have experience in this industry, so I will have a higher chance of success than most other entrepreneurs.

No doubt about it. Having prior experience in an industry will undoubtedly give you an advantage over a novice. The problem is that you probably don't have experience in *all aspects* of the given industry or business. You have probably worked in one or a few different areas in a particular business, not each part. Therefore, while you will know some parts very well, others will feel brand new.

For example, before I stepped out on my own, I had been in leadership roles in a property and casualty insurance company. I worked in technical accounting and even worked closely with the data and underwriting teams. However, I had never actually sold the product. When I decided to sell property and casualty insurance as part of my product offering, I realized I had no clue what I was doing! I had plenty of experience in insurance, but not in every area I would encounter.

It is the rarest of rare for someone to have prior experience in *every aspect* of their new business. As I have told many an entrepreneur, nothing is more humbling than going out on your own. However well you know an industry, you probably don't know everything! Many are surprised to realize the breadth of what they don't know.

Misconception 4: I will be able to live the same lifestyle I always have.

Bigger companies can afford more. It may seem unfair, but bigger companies have more to offer their employees. They can afford better healthcare benefits. A catered lunch or two is well within budget. If they have a bad month or two, their employees barely notice because the company can afford to buffer the impact.

When you go out on your own, it often comes with lifestyle sacrifices. In addition to giving more time to work, you typically need to live on less. You may not have the same healthcare right away. You may not be able to spend the same amount on vacation that you always have. If you have a retirement plan, the match may not be what you are used to. This is where your desire to do something different and pave your own way has to carry you. It won't be like this forever, but most businesses do not immediately take off. You can get these things back. It just may be a few years before you do. Patience and passion are essential when you embark on something new.

Misconception 5: Once I go out on my own, I will never look back.

Out of all the things on this list, this is the one that I wish most of all were true. While many movies paint the picture of the protagonist telling their boss to "shove it" and triumphantly walking out the door to be successful on their own without an ounce of self-doubt, real life is more complicated. In most cases, people go out on their own for a while, and the business has no other employees. It is just them. No one to help carry the load. While this can be empowering and allow for schedule flexibility, it can also be lonely and lead to self-doubt.

Many people have dipped their toe in the water of self-employment only to realize that the water was deeper than they thought. At some point, after an initial push, sales slow down, customers drag their feet in paying, and you run out of marketing ideas. This is where loneliness and fear can start to rear their ugly heads. You start to wonder, "What was I thinking?" And "I can try this again in a few years when I am more ready." And even "Wouldn't it be easier just to find another job at a different company?"

Moments of self-doubt are normal and should be expected. However, when you reach them, it is essential to take a step back, re-examine the situation, and do some self-reflection. Have you gotten to go? That is to say, are you at a point in your life where you *have* to know if you can do something on your own? If you are, then ask yourself if you answered that question. That is, have you found the answer is that you can't do this? Or are you just having a rough day? If it is the second one, you owe it to yourself to keep going. If it is the first one, maybe a return to corporate life is in your future. Either way is fine. Just make sure you have closure so you don't keep wondering about what could have been.

Make no mistake about it: Hollywood captures the American Dream of making it on your own. However, while the entrepreneurial spirit in the United States is alive and well, it takes much more than two hours and the cost of a large popcorn to actualize it.

Am I at go?

Have you reached the point where the urge to figure out if you could do something better outweighs the comfort of working in the same office every day? Are you irresistibly compelled to know if you can do it better? Have you reached the point where you just don't care if you fail, because the need to know if you can make it by yourself is that much stronger? If so, then you have gotten to go.

If you haven't gotten to go yet, reading the rest of this book will not help you get there. Nothing I say can help you reach go faster. You are either there or you are not. You are either at a point in your life where you can't bear the thought of not trying to go into business for yourself, or you are not. There really isn't an in-between. If you are in between and you try to step out on your own now, consciously or unconsciously, you probably won't give it everything you have. You will fall back into what is comfortable. So, if you haven't reached go yet, wait until you are there. Then come back to this book and keep reading.

If you have reached this point in your life, congratulations. You have taken a crucial first step. At this point, there is no turning back for you. You have much work ahead, but you are all in—and most importantly, you don't care. Passion is carrying you, and it will have to continue carrying you for the foreseeable future. Money won't do it because money will likely be tight for a while. A well-thought-out business plan won't do it because most first-year business plans get blown up anyway. Prestige won't do it either because your company may not be well-known for a while. Your passion will keep you going through the late hours. Your passion will keep you motivated when the sales don't seem to be coming. Your passion will drive you ahead. You just need to get to go . . . and go!

What's ahead?

This book is a practical guide for navigating those early years of being in business for yourself. It is not a book of pithy platitudes nor a treatise on how anyone can start a small business. I will be the first to tell you that nothing could be further from the truth. The fact is that not everyone can or should start their own business. However, if you are thinking about going out on your own, this book will help you get a handle on what is involved and what needs to happen over the next few years to accomplish that goal.

It should also be clear that this is not a step-by-step guide to starting a business, either. While there is logic to the order of the chapters, every company in every industry is different. Some steps may make more sense to do sooner rather than later. Realistically, most business owners must address many of these issues before they are ready. They also don't usually have the luxury of addressing these items in an orderly fashion. Starting a business is an exercise of addressing things that come up as best you can now and perfecting them later.

Also, in case you are wondering, I am not an attorney. This book should never be construed as legal advice. If you need legal advice on a specific issue, hire a competent attorney. If you need an expert in tax, insurance, or human resources, hire a professional. This book cannot address every situation or problem. I don't try to because I can't.

In many ways, this book is my essay on everything I have learned from starting several businesses over time, not with the deep pockets of investors, but out of my own wallet. It is not from the viewpoint of someone trying to sell a do-it-yourself marketing strategy, nor from the point of view of a small business strategist at a large financial firm who has only seen businesses built from the sidelines. It is a book from someone who has made plenty of mistakes but managed to have a few victories along the way. This is simply a book from one passionate entrepreneur to another in hopes that you will be able to realize your dream of making it on your own as well.

CHAPTER 1

It's Not a Suggestion: You Need to Register

NOTE: This chapter provides no legal advice about where a company needs to register. I am not an attorney, so these are merely observations and helpful suggestions based on what I have encountered in my business career. Nothing more. Also, laws change from time to time. If you have questions about current regulations related to your specific situation and business, you should talk to a licensed attorney in your state.

Getting my driver's license was a passport to freedom. The ability to go places on my own without supervision changed my perspective. It brought out my independence. It brought out my sense of adventure. Unfortunately, it also brought out my lead foot!

On one night, I remember getting pulled over by a police officer after picking up a friend of mine. When I saw the lights in my rearview mirror, a sick feeling emerged in the pit of my stomach. As someone who never really got in trouble, I was devastated. I had no excuse. I just made the mistake of enjoying my freedom a bit too much and not paying attention to the speedometer. All the same, I will never forget the police officer's question to me as he looked into the car: "Did you think the speed limit sign was a suggestion?"

His question was a bit sarcastic, but perfectly appropriate in the circumstances. His point was simple: there are certain things you just do. You do them because society, regulators, or even local law enforcement require you to. By doing these things, society runs smoother, and you save yourself a lot of headaches later on.

Perhaps this is why I lose patience quickly with small business owners who argue about registration requirements or business licensing. They question why the laws exist. They ask if there are ways to get around them. I have even had one or two talk about the fairness or legality of the requirements. While these might be interesting philosophical discussions, the reality of the situation is much simpler: if you want to do business in a state, you need to register. Depending on your business, you may need a business license as well. Without doing these things, you have no business. It really is that simple.

How do I register?

In most states, you can register with the Secretary of State on the state's website, in person, or by mail. The state will want to know some basic information about the company, including what services or products the company provides. In most states, you can either register yourself or have an attorney help you. The state normally charges the company a fee. If you want the state to process your registration faster, you may be able to pay an expedited fee. This can be worth it if you want to start selling your product or service quickly. Most of the time, the actual application for registration is not terribly long, but it can be confusing, which is where an attorney can help.

Do I have to register everywhere?

You must in the state where you are located, but you also need to register in all states where you are "doing business." The problem is that there is not one consistent definition of what constitutes "doing business." If you are selling to clients or providing services (like physically traveling over state lines to do a job), then you almost certainly have to register in that state. Yet, with the rise of Internet sales, it is not unusual for even an online business to have to register in multiple states—the state your business is based from, as well as any other state it is doing business in.

One common exception to the rules regarding registration is for sole proprietorships. If your business is formed as a sole proprietorship, you may not need to register with the state. However, even in the case of a sole proprietorship, you may still have to register to obtain a business license, open a checking account, or otherwise operate in a state. It is never a good idea to assume you don't have to register. Most businesses do. You should expect to have to do it as well.

If I register in a state, do I have to pay taxes there?

Technically, whether you need to register in a state and whether you need to pay taxes are two different questions. However, it is rare for someone doing business in a state and registered there not to have to file a tax return there as well. It is more common to pay taxes in every state where you are registered in. We will talk more about taxes later.

Do I need a business license?

There are certain industries and professions where a business license is required. For example, a federal license may be required for agricultural activities, firearms, or aviation-based businesses. You may also need a state license to run a hair salon, accounting firm, or law office. Localities also have licensing requirements. For example, a restaurant may need a permit or license to sell alcohol. However, if you are not running a business that requires a special license, then no, you normally don't need one.

If you are unsure, many states provide information for new businesses on the Secretary of State or Department of Taxation's websites. The types of businesses needing a license are often listed for you. It is important to remember that even if you are small, you still need a license. Business licenses are required based on what you do, not how big your business is.

Is business registration the same as formation?

Not exactly. To form a business, you often need to file formation papers with the state where you want to be formed. Formation papers are exactly what they sound like—they are filed to create the entity. For example, to start a corporation, you generally must file Articles of Incorporation. To start a limited liability company (LLC), you normally have to file Articles of Organization. Here are some of the common formation papers:

- Articles of Incorporation—These are filed to form a corporation.
- Articles of Organization—These are filed to form a Limited Liability Company.

- Certificate of Limited Partnership—These are filed to form a limited partnership.

Registration is the process of filing paperwork with the state where you want to do business. You might register with a state after you have already formed. For example, I might form my business in Virginia by filing Articles of Organization. I might need to register in North Carolina, too, if I am doing business there. When you register outside of your resident state, this is sometimes called a foreign registration. But I wouldn't form in North Carolina again; I already did that in Virginia.

As my grandmother would say, don't get tangled up on the names. Some states call things by slightly different names. When you register in your home state, it may be called a domestic registration or a resident registration. Don't worry about that part. If you get confused, look on the website and read the descriptions on what each form is designed to do. If all else fails, call someone at the Secretary of State's office. I have found that many Secretary of State workers are happy when someone calls to verify the form they are supposed to use. After all, it saves them the headache of rejecting paperwork multiple times!

The bottom line is that formation and registration are similar in some ways, but not the same thing. You only form once, but you may need to register many times in multiple states. In either case, you are filing paperwork in a state to notify the state that you plan on conducting business there. This makes your business actions legal and tells the state you are there.

What about federal taxes?

Once your formation papers have been filed with the Secretary of State, you will need to obtain a tax ID (employer identification number or EIN) from the IRS. This can be done on the IRS website (www.irs.gov). The IRS will ask you to fill out information about your business, including the entity type, when you started your business, and if you expect to have payroll. As long as you have all of the information available, the online process is usually quick, generating an automatic letter that assigns your business's EIN. You must keep this letter, since you will need it for many things (including when registering with the state taxing authorities—see below).

Even if you plan on forming a sole proprietorship, you may still need an EIN. For example, an EIN is often required to open a business checking account. It may also be needed for insurance or entering into contracts with potential customers and vendors.

What about the state taxing authorities?

In addition to registering with the Secretary of State, many states will require you to register with the State Department of Taxation. This can typically be done online. Once you set up an account for your business, you will be taken through a questionnaire asking about your business. This helps the department figure out which taxes the entity will be filing. For example, not all entities will be subject to sales tax or personal property tax, but nearly all will be subject to income taxes. Once the questionnaire is filled out, the state may issue you a unique state tax ID that needs to be shown on all the returns you file. In many cases, a tax return will not be accepted if the entity does not have a state tax ID. It also may take some time to process the paperwork of a new entity. Therefore, it is usually best to register with the state taxing authorities early on.

What is a legal vs. a trade name?

When you form your business by filing paperwork with the Secretary of State, you will need to enter a company name on the paperwork. This is your legal name. State laws will vary regarding what your name can be. Generally, a company's name can't be confusingly similar to that of another company already in the state.

Also, it is usually required for a business to identify how it is organized in its name. For example, let's say I want to form a company called ABC as an LLC. The state might require me to have a legal name of ABC, LLC. If I wanted it to be a corporation, I would need to call it ABC, Inc. or ABC Corporation. In any of these instances, I could not just call it ABC. I would need to identify the company's entity type in the name.

Additionally, certain industries may require specific identifiers in a company's legal name. At one point in my career, I worked for a startup insurance agency. In some states, we needed to indicate that we were an insurance agency in our legal name. Therefore, our legal name was Compare.com Insurance Agency, LLC.

Since legal names can be rather cumbersome (and not very attractive to put on business cards), businesses can also file a trade name—also called a doing business as (DBA) or fictitious name. This is the name the company will use in its advertising, storefront, and on business cards. For example, the company's legal name may be ABC, LLC, but its trade name is just ABC. Trade names are meant to be more marketable and brand-oriented than legal names.

Trade names are typically registered with a state or county. However, filing a trade name in one county does not necessarily allow me to use that trade name across the United States. Trade names are usually only good for the area in which they are filed.[3]

FINCEN Reporting

Once you have formed your business, you may need to register it with the Financial Crimes Enforcement Network (FINCEN) if you have any foreign owners or started the business outside the United States.[4] For each entity required to report, you will generally be asked for the following information:

- Legal name
- Any trade names, "doing business as," or "trading as" names
- Current street address of the principal place of business
- Jurisdiction of formation or registration
- Taxpayer Identification Number

In addition, each entity subject to reporting will also need to report its beneficial owners. Beneficial owners are basically the owners of a business or anyone who exercises control over the business (like a Chief Operating Officer or Chief Executive Officer).[5] For each beneficial owner, the following information will generally be reported:

- The individual's name, date of birth, and residential street

3 If you have concerns about where you can and cannot use your business's trade name, you should talk to an attorney who has a deep knowledge of various states' business laws.

4 See FINCEN Interim Final Rule (March 26, 2025)

5 The term used on the FINCEN website is "substantial control." It is important to note that not only company owners are beneficial owners; other key employees may be beneficial owners as well.

address (not a business address)

- A unique identifying number from an acceptable identification document (like an unexpired driver's license or passport), along with an image of the document
- The name of the state or jurisdiction that issued the identification document

The company will also need to report information on who helped them file formation papers with the Secretary of State. These individuals are referred to as "Company Applicants."

This is obviously a lot of information! However, for foreign owners and foreign businesses hoping to do business in the United States, it is important for this filing not to get lost in the shuffle. There are significant fines for missing this filing!

Zoning

If you have an office, you usually need to apply for a zoning permit before your new company can begin operations. Zoning permits are typically given at the local level. For example, a city will provide a zoning permit to a business so it may operate within the jurisdiction of the city. You usually have to fill out an application and provide certain information about your office before you will be granted a permit.

These days, it is not unusual for a new business owner to start a business without having a physical office. For example, they may start the business from their kitchen table with only a laptop. It is important to remember that zoning generally applies to all businesses, even home-based ones. Many jurisdictions have a more streamlined zoning process for home-based businesses. However, the company still has to apply for a permit (even if you really are just getting a permit to use your own living room or kitchen table).

The Business Checking Account

While this chapter is mainly about getting set up from a compliance and regulatory perspective, it is hard to do this without paying fees. You pay numerous fees upfront to get a business started: a fee to file your formation papers, a fee for your zoning permit, a fee to get your business license, and so on. You need to keep track of these fees for your tax accountant anyway (more on this later), and tracking these costs is much easier if everything is running through a business checking account. Then all your business transactions will be separate from your personal ones. They will be easy to identify. For this reason, you generally want to get a business checking account open as soon as possible.

When you open your business checking account, the bank will ask you for the company's legal name and tax ID. Therefore, you need to complete these steps first (see below for a suggested order of how to do things). While there is nothing wrong with opening a new account online, it can be easier to walk into a branch office and talk to a real person. They can usually help you identify what you are missing more quickly and answer any questions you might have on the spot. When you go to the bank branch, bring your formation papers from the Secretary of State and your EIN confirmation letter from the IRS. They may still need something else from you, but these items will almost certainly be required. If you have everything, they can open an account for you in a few minutes.

When trying to figure out what bank to open a business checking account with, I typically tell clients to first look at the deals that their personal bank offers. Sometimes, if you are a personal banking customer, the bank may offer a deal on business checking. Also, pay attention to account minimums and fees. Sometimes, a bank will charge a fee if your account balance falls below a certain amount (often called a minimum balance fee). Maintaining a high minimum balance does nothing but tie up cash, which usually hinders a small business owner. Therefore, try to find an account with low or no minimum balance requirements. Also, look at where they have ATMs and branches. Try to ensure that the bank you choose has a presence in the areas where you are likely to be conducting business (meeting with clients, performing work, etc.). If you need something from your bank, you don't want to scramble to find a branch!

Suggested Order

Whenever I meet new clients, they are often overwhelmed by what I have laid out in this chapter. Undoubtedly, taking care of these regulatory requirements takes time and money. The most common question is, "What do I do first?" Here is my suggested ordering:

- File your formation papers with the Secretary of State.
- Once your formation papers have been approved, file your Form SS-4 with the IRS to get your EIN (tax ID).
- Open your business checking account.
- Report your beneficial owners to FINCEN (if necessary)
- Apply for your Trade Name (if you need one).
- Apply for your business license (if you need one).
- Apply for zoning.
- Register in other states/jurisdictions if necessary.
- Get business licenses and zoning in other states/jurisdictions if necessary.

Keep in mind that every state is different. Some state laws or procedures may dictate that you do these steps in a slightly different order. For example, you may need to complete your zoning application before applying for a business license. The above is only meant as a general guide.

Tips for Getting to Go

1. Never begin selling your product or service before checking whether you need a business license. Depending on the industry you are in, the penalties can be stiff. You want your business to have a chance to get off the ground, and getting in trouble for doing business without a license will kill your idea quickly!
2. Try to get the applications for each item outlined above done quickly, since you will need to wait for approval by the appropriate agency (Secretary of State, IRS, Zoning Board, etc.). I typically tell clients to aim to have all the applications submitted to the relevant agencies in a week or two. You need to move quickly, because you can't really start your business until these steps are done.
3. It is not unusual to have initial problems with an application to a regulatory agency. This can be frustrating, especially when you are excited to start your business. You need to be patient with both the process and the people involved. Part of the reason the United States is such a great place to do business is because of all the laws we have in place. Our system is imperfect but reliable and attempts to be as transparent as possible. So, be patient! It will get done. Work through the steps, and you will be up and going as soon as possible. (When you are successful later, you can look back and laugh!)

4. As I mentioned, I am not an attorney. This chapter only gives you a general outline of things you may need to look into. You should always consult with an attorney regarding legal issues in your state, current laws, and your specific situation.

CHAPTER 2

Tying Yourself in Knots: You Need an Entity

I distinctly remember sitting in the back of a CPA continuing education course and listening to an experienced and well-meaning tax attorney discuss the ins and outs of various entity types. After several hours of lecture, questions, and discussion, he finally summed up his talk by saying, "Always have the end in mind when talking to clients about entity type. By talking to them about their exit plan, you can avoid costly mistakes along the way."

Around the room, some practitioners were nodding their heads approvingly as if they had just reached a moment of enlightenment. In my mind, I thought, "That's the stupidest thing I have ever heard." Getting a business off the ground is hard enough. And this guy wanted us to ask our clients what their exit plan was up front to get the best financial result? How stressful for the client! On top of everything else new business owners have to deal with, this guy wanted them to think about their exit plan, too?

I have jokingly told clients that I would be the best financial advisor in the universe if only I could predict the future. If you can predict the future, then all of your decisions (business and otherwise) will be perfect. You will be able to see changes and problems before they happen. But as my grandmother would say, "That's not how life works." We don't know what's up ahead. That's part of the endless challenge (and excitement) of being in business for yourself. You roll with the punches and adjust to changes as they come. You can tie yourself in knots trying to think of all the what ifs.

This is not to say you shouldn't think ahead at all. Some forethought is helpful, but too much forethought can paralyze your thinking. When it comes to picking an entity type, I think this is especially important to keep in mind. While certain advantages and disadvantages are inherent in each entity type, it is impossible to think of everything. So don't try. Think about what you know about your business now and make the best choice for now. If things change down the road, you can adjust later.

Stand-Alone Entities vs. Pass-Through Entities

From a tax perspective, there are two categories of entities: stand-alone entities and pass-through entities. Stand-alone entities file their own returns and pay their own taxes. They have their own tax rate, which may be very different from the tax rate paid by the business owner. Currently, the only type of stand-alone entity is the C corporation.

In contrast, pass-through entities generally do not pay their own taxes, nor do they have their own tax rate.[6] They may or may not file their own tax return. They simply pass the income and deductions earned by the entity to the business owners. The business owners then pay the taxes on the business income at their personal income tax rate. Pass-through entities include sole proprietorships, partnerships, and S corporations.

Let's say that a business with two equal owners earns $100,000. If the business is organized as a C corporation (a stand-alone entity), the business would file its own tax return. On the return, it would show the income and pay taxes on it at the corporate tax rate. The owners would not show any income from the business on their own tax returns. They would only show the wages they earned from working, their investment income, and any other personal income. They would also show their personal deductions. They would pay their respective personal income tax rates on this income. The business pays taxes on the business income, and the owners pay taxes on their personal income. Straightforward enough.

On the other hand, if the entity was set up as a partnership (a pass-through entity), the business would still file a tax return but not pay any taxes. The items of income and deduction from the business would be split between the two business owners (50/50 in our example, since they are equal business owners) and shown on their personal returns. Let's say that one business owner had a personal tax rate of 22%, while the other had a personal tax rate of 32%. The first business owner would pay taxes on their half of the business income

---

6 There are some instances in which a pass-through entity may have to pay its own taxes. For example, an S corporation may be responsible for paying the built-in gains tax or the excess passive income tax. Partnerships and S corporations may have to pay state income taxes as well. However, these situations are not the norm and are beyond the scope of this discussion. If you want more information about these instances, talk to your financial advisor or tax practitioner.

at a 22% rate. The second business owner would pay taxes on their half of the business income at 32%.

It should be noted that a business owner can have a higher or lower tax rate than the corporate tax rate. Also, as seen above, different owners of the same business may pay taxes at different rates.

What is a sole proprietorship?

A sole proprietorship is a pass-through entity owned by one person. It is by far the easiest to set up because it often does not need to register with the Secretary of State.[7] You may need a business license to get started, but there are no formal documents to file. You simply hang your shingle outside and get started. This is certainly appealing when you have a new idea. You can get started fast, and that's probably the biggest advantage to sole proprietorships. You can also pull money out of the business and put money into it without any tax consequences. Plus, you don't need to file a separate federal tax return.[8] All of your business income and deductions are summarized and shown as part of your personal income tax return. Sole proprietorships are simple and have minimal (if any) organizational costs.

However, they also have several downsides. First, sole proprietorships have unlimited liability. Creditors can generally go after the individual's personal assets if the business cannot pay its bills. Second, sole proprietorships must pay self-employment taxes. This means that, in addition to regular income taxes, a sole proprietor must pay both employer and employee payroll taxes on the business's

---

7 As we said in the chapter on registration, this depends on what profession you are in. Some businesses still need to register with a regulatory authority, even if they are a sole proprietorship. For example, a CPA firm generally still must register with the state board of accountancy even if it is organized as a sole proprietorship.

8 Some states may require a separate tax return for a sole proprietorship.

net profit.

If you have ever looked at your paycheck, you will notice that you pay Social Security (or FICA) and Medicare taxes. Social Security taxes are assessed at 6.2% of your wage income, while Medicare taxes are 1.45% of this same income. These are taxes that every employee pays. In addition to this, your employer pays a matching amount on each employee's wages as well.

When you are sole proprietor, you are both an employer and an employee. Therefore, you pay both the employer and employee sides of Social Security and Medicare taxes on your business profit (business income minus business expenses). This results in a 15.3% tax (6.2% + 6.2% + 1.45% + 1.45% = 15.3%) that is often referred to as self-employment taxes.

What makes this worse yet is that this is on top of your regular income taxes. Imagine you are a sole proprietor, and your personal tax rate is 22%. If you had a business profit of $100,000, you would pay $15,300 in self-employment taxes *and* $22,000 in regular income taxes! In my experience, self-employment taxes tend to take many small business owners by surprise. They don't realize how much they must pay until they receive a huge tax bill at the end of the year.

When considering whether to form a sole proprietorship, you need to weigh the ease of setup and the ability to pull money without tax consequences against the potentially damaging effects of self-employment taxes and unlimited liability. As many businesses mature and income and assets increase, the concern over self-employment taxes and liability becomes too great. Therefore, they look for an entity type that can lessen the damaging effects of these two items.

What is a partnership?

A partnership is another pass-through entity that has two or more business owners. Unlike a sole proprietorship, a partnership must file its own tax return (a Form 1065 for federal tax purposes). The partnership does not pay taxes, so Form 1065 merely shows the total income and deductions for the business for the tax year. Each partner then receives a Schedule K-1 reflecting their share of the business's income and deductions for the year. This form tells them what they need to show on their tax return. A copy is given to each partner (the business owners) as well as the IRS.

Partners do not have to share the income and expenses of the business equally. They can share their income and deductions in another way that they agree upon. For example, the partners might decide to share 75/25. They could also agree to share certain income and deductions differently. For instance, they might agree to share depreciation 70/30, but all other income and deductions 50/50. It should be noted that the IRS limits how items may be shared. For the IRS to respect a special allocation of income or deduction, it generally must have "substantial economic effect." These rules are very complex. Therefore, while partnerships provide a significant amount of flexibility, you will likely need the assistance of a tax accountant or attorney if you get into more complex sharing structures.[9]

Like sole proprietorships, partners must be concerned with liability and self-employment taxes. A partnership can generally include two different types of partners: general partners and limited partners. General partners are involved in the business's day-to-day

9 The complexity of partnership tax law should not be underestimated. Let's say that you want to share depreciation differently all of your other deductions. You would need an attorney to draft a partnership agreement to reflect this desire and a competent tax accountant to help you make sure this situation will be deemed to have substantial economic effect. You just need to make sure the tax advantages outweigh the costs of hiring these outside professionals.

activities. They can help manage the business's affairs, enter into contracts, and perform services for customers. Like sole proprietors, they have unlimited liability. Their share of any income from the partnership is also generally subject to self-employment taxes.[10]

The other type of partner is a limited partner. Limited partners are more like investors in that they often provide capital to the partnership, but they may not participate in the business's day-to-day activities. Unlike general partners, limited partners have limited liability. In other words, creditors may be able to take the money and assets that they contribute to the partnership, but nothing more. While creditors can come after the personal assets of a general partner, they usually cannot do this to a limited partner. Limited partners also do not have to worry about self-employment taxes on their share of the partnership's income.

The only exception to this is for guaranteed payments. If a limited partner is paid a fixed amount (unrelated to the partnership's performance) for their services, this payment type is subject to self-employment taxes. For example, let's say that a limited partner is paid $50,000 for their consulting services. This $50,000 payment is guaranteed whether the partnership makes or loses money. That $50,000 payment would be subject to self-employment taxes. However, any share of the partnership's income that *is* based on whether the partnership makes money would not be subject to self-employment taxes.

A partnership with only general partners is referred to as a general partnership. It is referred to as a limited partnership when it has both limited and general partners.[11]

---

10 There are certain types of income that by their nature are not subject to self-employment taxes. For example, a partnership's rental income, interest income, and dividend income are normally not subject to self-employment taxes. However, the income that a partnership earns from selling its product or service is subject to self-employment taxes.

11 A limited partnership must have at least one general partner. There is no way to form a partnership with all limited partners. However, see the section on LLCs below for more details.

While it is possible to form a partnership without a written partnership agreement, this is not a good idea. Even families and friends who are very close fight occasionally, so putting the entire agreement in writing is best. A partnership agreement will include how items of income and deduction are shared by the partners for tax purposes, what each partner gets if the partnership liquidates, and what legal rights each partner has. In short, a partnership agreement tells each partner what to expect in the arrangement. While you could draft your partnership agreement, it is usually better to have an attorney do this. It is a very valuable and important document to have in place.

What is an S corporation?

An S corporation may be owned by one or more persons and is another type of flow-through entity. Many states do not recognize S corporations as a type of entity under the law. The Secretary of State often treats an S corporation just like any other C corporation. That is to say, the state will treat them all as corporations and subject them to the laws of corporations. It is best to think about an S corporation as a special way to tax a corporation rather than as a distinct entity type for legal purposes.[12] S corporations are a tax thing. Nothing more.

S corporations file their own tax return (Form 1120-S at the federal level). Like the partnership return, the Form 1120-S merely summarizes all of the income and deductions for the business. With a few exceptions, S corporations do not pay taxes. Like the other pass-through entities, each S corporation shareholder takes their share of the S corporation's income and deductions on their personal tax return. Like a partnership, each S corporation shareholder receives a

12 It is possible for an LLC to elect to be treated like an S corporation for tax purposes as well. More on this later.

Schedule K-1, which shows their share of the income and deductions from the S corporation. They pay taxes on their share of income and deductions at their individual tax rate.

S Corporation vs. Partnership

While there are several similarities between S corporations and partnerships, there are also some key differences. In both cases, the business can typically distribute money and property to the owners without paying taxes. However, the tax code limits this. If too much income is distributed from either a partnership or an S corporation to the business owner, the business owner may have to declare more income on their individual tax return.

One key difference between the two is how items of income and deduction may be shared amongst the owners. Partners can decide to share income and deductions differently. For example, a partner may be able to take 100% of the depreciation of the entity but only 50% of all other deductions. An S corporation shareholder could not do this. S corporation shareholders must take items of income and deductions in proportion to their ownership interest. For example, a 25% S corporation shareholder would need to take 25% of all S corporation income and deductions.

Also, while someone who is not from the United States can own a share of a partnership, they cannot do this with an S corporation. S corporations can only have US owners and may only have up to one hundred owners.

What is a C corporation?

Unlike the other entity types we discussed, a C corporation is a stand-alone entity for tax purposes. In other words, C corporations file their own tax returns and pay their own taxes. None of the income and deductions from the business are shown on the owners' personal tax returns. The business pays its own income taxes at the corporate tax rate. Shareholders of a C corporation also have limited liability. In other words, while the company's creditors can take anything they have invested in the business, they may not take the shareholders' personal assets.

There are very few restrictions on who may own a C corporation or how many owners there can be. A C corporation can be owned by one person or thousands of people. Those owners may be US residents or residents of another country. Also, while there can be some restrictions on the type of benefits that may be paid to an owner of a flow-through entity, there are very few limitations for owners of a C corporation. In other words, a C corporation owner is generally entitled to the same benefits paid to any employee. If a partnership or S corporation paid for the health insurance of its owner, the owner would need to pay taxes on this amount on their personal tax return. However, the owner of a C corporation can have their health insurance paid for by the company and not have to pay any personal taxes on this amount.

Perhaps the biggest drawback to C corporations, however, is how dividends are taxed. Distributions from a C corporation are not deductible by the corporation. However, they are taxable to the shareholders who receive them on the individual tax return. This creates what is often referred to as "double taxation." For example, let's say that a corporation has $100,000 of taxable income and it pays a $10,000 dividend to its only shareholder. Since dividends are not deductible, the corporation would still pay taxes on $100,000 of income. Additionally, the shareholder would pay personal taxes on the $10,000 dividend on his/her personal return. The dividend essentially gets taxed twice: once at the entity level, since dividends are not deductible, and again at the individual tax level.

Another potential disadvantage is corporate governance. Corporations must normally draft bylaws, hold shareholder meetings, and are generally subject to more administrative requirements than other entities. This can be a lot for a small business owner to handle!

What is a limited liability company?

Perhaps the most popular type of entity structure among small business owners is the LLC. An LLC provides limited liability for all the entity's owners, similar to limited partners in a limited partnership. However, unlike limited partners, LLC members (the owners of an LLC) can participate in the day-to-day management activities of the business. In this way, they have the best of both worlds—limited risk but the ability to be a part of the business operations.

From a tax perspective, LLCs also have a lot of flexibility. They can generally choose how they want to be taxed. If there is one business owner (LLC member) with no elections, an LLC is taxed like a sole proprietorship, and net income is generally subject to self-employment taxes. However, the business owner may elect to be treated like a C corporation for tax purposes by filing Form 8832. If they do this, the LLC would file a Form 1120, just like any other C corporation, and pay its own taxes. The business owner may also elect to be treated like an S corporation by filing Form 2553. They would then file an 1120-S like any other S corporation.

If more than one person owns the LLC and no elections are made, then the LLC is treated like a partnership. It will file a Form 1065. An LLC with multiple owners may also elect to be treated like a C corporation or S corporation. It should be noted that this flexibility is not unlimited. Once an LLC decides on how it wants to be taxed, it generally must stick with it for five years.[13] An entity cannot switch back and forth between entity types from one year to the next. However, this flexibility can be ideal for a small business owner who doesn't know what the future holds. They can gain liability protection by forming as an LLC and then figure out how they want to be taxed as the business grows and adapts.

The downside to LLCs is primarily in the ambiguity of the tax law. Since LLCs essentially take on the tax attributes of the entity they choose to be taxed like, it may be difficult to discern which tax laws apply. Therefore, an LLC owner will likely need the help of a tax professional.

Do I really have to choose?

When considering all the characteristics of the different entities, it may be tempting not to make a choice. In a meeting once, a new client of mine became so overwhelmed by what type of business entity to choose that he put his face in his hands and just shook his head for several minutes!

The problem is that by not making a choice, the IRS essentially makes you choose. If I am the only owner of my business and I don't file anything with the Secretary of State or the IRS, my business is treated like a sole proprietorship. I still have to declare the income

13 There are several exceptions in the tax law to this five-year rule. The bottom line is that it is not normally possible to change your entity anytime you want. The IRS limits how often and when you can switch.

on my personal income tax return on Schedule C. Similarly, if others own my business in addition to me, my business is treated like a general partnership for tax purposes. My advice is simple: if you do nothing, the IRS will choose an entity type for you, so you might as well be proactive and choose for yourself. The key is to realize that there is no such thing as a perfect choice, you just have to make one.

In terms of getting out of the business, ownership interests in certain entity types indeed have various tax advantages and disadvantages. Partnerships have complicated look-through provisions that can make business owners pay more taxes.[14] A sale of a sole proprietorship is seen as the sale of assets individually in many cases. Sales of C corporation shares can be easy, but care must be taken when redeeming shares to ensure the rules are met to avoid unwanted tax effects.[15] The list goes on. Every move has downsides, so all you can do is make the best decision you can now with what you think the business will do. No one knows what the future will hold, and too much analysis at the beginning stages of a business will often only make your head spin!

A mentor once told me that building a business was often an exercise in humility. He meant that new business owners often learn how much they don't know as they grow. You hardly, if ever, have all the information; you just make the best choice you can in the circumstances. So, make a choice! Then move on—you have other things to do!

---

14 Sec 751 and several others may apply; these change the tax rate to something higher than the capital gains rate.

15 Sec 302 redemption treatment rules are very specific. If the redemption rules are not met, then a redemption could be treated like a dividend.

Tips for Getting to Go

1. Limited Liability Companies tend to be easy to form and provide some liability protection. If you are looking for flexibility in terms of how the entity is taxed, this may be the best choice.
2. If you want to be sure you can pay yourself fringe benefits without significant tax complications, then a C corporation may be the best choice. If fringe benefits are paid to the owner of an S corporation or partnership, the fringe benefits must generally be taken as compensation on the owners' individual tax return.[16] C corporation owners don't have to do this.
3. If you don't want the hassle or expense of filing a separate business tax return, then the only options are a sole proprietorship or a single-member LLC. You should consider your liability if you do this, though. Also, those self-employment taxes can creep up fast!

---

16 Fringe benefits are shown as additional W-2 income for an S corporation owner. For partners, fringe benefit payments are taxed as a guaranteed payment.

CHAPTER 3

Spinning Plates: You Need a Marketing Plan

Before I went out on my own, I was the first Chief Financial Officer at Compare.com, a startup price comparison website for auto insurance rates, which was located in the Richmond, Virginia area. As part of this role, I would periodically travel to Cardiff, Wales, to participate in meetings with other CFOs from affiliate companies worldwide under our mutual parent company. A few months into the job, I was at one of these meetings with my fellow CFOs, taking part in a unique team-building event that involved each of us showing our skills as circus performers. A company in the Cardiff area routinely taught leadership skills by teaching executives how to juggle clubs, trust another to catch them when flying through the air on a flying trapeze, and even perform improvisational jokes as a clown might do. Amid the chaos and laughter that inevitably ensued, I still remember a profound message that came to me while trying (unsuccessfully) to spin multiple plates simultaneously. You can plan all you want, but business strategy often involves adaptation and a willingness to break from the plan to ensure things stay on the right track. Let me explain.

When most people try to spin plates like a circus performer would, they start by getting the first plate going and then moving on to the next one. You do this for each plate until you have them all spinning. At this point, the first plate is starting to lose momentum, and you need to return to it. However, you can easily move right down the line again and again and again. Simple, right?

All of this sounds logical, but anyone who has spun plates before will tell you that this approach has a flaw. You assume that the momentum you build on each plate is equal and predictable. You think you can get each plate going before you need to circle back to the first and that you will be able to attend to this first plate before you must attend to the second one. In reality, you don't get all the plates going at the same speed. Some plates lose momentum faster than others, so you have to make decisions. Do I have enough time to start this plate? Or do I need to circle back to that one plate that seems to be losing speed? Or, if I have two plates losing speed at the same time, which one do I go to first?

In short, success at spinning plates necessarily involves attending to issues as they come up and shifting on the fly. The sure way to fail at this exercise is to be overly committed to a logical and orderly flow of operations, assuming you will only have to move from one plate to another. The only way to be successful at spinning plates is to make good decisions about which plates need your attention and which ones you can leave alone for a bit longer. Business strategy and marketing are similar. You can't be everywhere, so you must prioritize what needs your attention and what you can let go.

Shouldn't I perfect my product before marketing?

I have always been a perfectionist and organizer at heart. (After all, I did go into tax accounting!) I like to have everything completed with one task before moving on to the next. I have heard many entrepreneurs try to approach their new business this way. They want to get everything set up and perfect the product before they do anything on the marketing side. The problem is that in most cases, like spinning plates, the world simply won't let you do this. You can have a business that is completely set up—product testing is done, software is bought, and the tax entity is formed. However, if you have not done any marketing during the setup process, it will be even longer before you sell anything. You actually slow down the process of establishing your business and making the first sale by trying to be too organized. You must do both.

We should be clear here. There are some things that the law requires before you start marketing your business. For example, you may have to obtain a state registration and business license before marketing to the public (see the first chapter). Also, you need at least some product development before offering that product or service to the public. There are some things that must happen before you begin generating interest in your business. The problem is when you try to have *everything* perfect before advertising.

At a former job, I had a mentor who used to say, "Perfect is the enemy of the good." This saying is credited to Voltaire, an eighteenth-century French philosopher, but I first heard it from my former boss, Andrew. Whenever he said that phrase, he meant that if you wait for perfection, you will never move on to the next phase. At one point, Andrew used this phrase when talking about our company website. The web designers kept coming up with laundry lists of items that needed to be fixed on the site. Andrew kept telling them, "Perfect is the enemy of the good." He meant that at some point, we had to make our website live. Until we did, it was no good to us. It was just a project that was not driving sales.

Any business must be presented to the public, which means that marketing and operational setup often need to be done simultaneously. You spin plates and attend to what needs to be done at that given moment. We will talk about compliance and other operational setup issues later. Now, let's discuss the marketing setup. This all starts with developing a marketing plan.

What is a marketing plan?

A marketing plan generally identifies the target customer and how you plan on reaching them. An outline of a marketing plan should touch on both strategic and operational components.

Strategic Components

1. **SWOT (Strengths, Weaknesses, Opportunities, and Threats)** —Make a list of each of the following:
2. **Strengths:** What are the strengths you believe your business has? If the business has already started, what strengths have contributed to your success so far?
3. **Weaknesses:** What are some areas you anticipate your business will struggle with? Can you do anything to mitigate these struggles, or are these inherent weaknesses with your model?
4. **Opportunities:** What are you in a unique position to accomplish? Are there certain things you believe you can do better than any other business? What are they?

5. **Threats:** What may prevent you from doing what you want in the market? Can you identify any barriers to success?
6. **Market Analysis**: How many potential customers are there, and what are their demographics, common careers, income levels, etc.? In other words, what is the potential business?
7. **Value Proposition**: What differentiates your product or service from any others? What is the value you bring? If there are eight other businesses just like yours on the same street, how will you stand out?
8. **Marketing Strategy Objectives**: What are you trying to accomplish with your marketing?
9. **Customer Understanding and Buyer Personas**: Being all things to all people is tough and usually not possible. A buyer persona is a fictionalized version of your target customer. By visualizing your key customer, you can better figure out how to identify them. So, who is your product or service aimed at? What are your customers looking for? What are their problems? How do you offer a solution?

Operational Components

1. **Budget**: Your marketing spend should be broken down by channel. Do you want to spend money on email marketing? If so, how much? What about your website? Direct mailing?
2. **Evaluation of Success**: You need to consider what success looks like for your marketing, ideally with quantitative metrics. For a new business, an abundance of new sales may not be possible right away. It may be more realistic to base your initial marketing goals on the number of new client meetings, website views, or even the number of new contacts made.

The Problem with Marketing Plans

As seen above, marketing plans will typically start with analyzing the potential market size and basic characteristics—the number of women and men, median income level, and number of people in each household. The idea is to think about the potential size of your audience realistically. If your product is a toy made for preschool-age children, there should be enough preschool-age children in a particular area to justify your time and effort. If there are not, you should reevaluate where you plan to spend your money.

Next, you must figure out how to reach your potential audience. Some marketing methods are more expensive than others. You generally want to spend money on the one that will give you the most "bang for your buck." For example, while sending emails to a list of people is generally cheap, open rates tend to be low. If no one actually sees your email, it may be a waste of time and money. In contrast, TV advertising can be expensive and cost prohibitive. Also, it usually takes repeated exposure to a product before many people will decide to buy it. Therefore, the question then becomes, can you get enough advertising on TV to make it worth your while and gain the attention you need? Whatever method you choose, your marketing plan should objectively estimate what part of the market you reasonably think you can capture. You can then figure out your cost per sale. Price your product at something more than your cost per sale, and presto! You now have a successful business!

This all sounds straightforward, but the cold dose of reality is that it is never that simple, and most marketing plans get blown up . Even if you do your best to think about how people might react to your product ahead of time, it is hard to predict sales, response rates, and even the cost of sales. For this reason, the marketing plans of many small business owners tend to go in the garbage pretty quickly. So, what's the solution? Don't be married to your marketing plan!

Marketing Plans Need Contingencies

Let me be clear: I am not saying that marketing plans are a waste of time. However, in many cases, their value lies in the process of putting them together and the questions they bring up, not what they actually say. Think about it. Before you invest your time and money into a business, you should figure out if there is potential to sell anything. You may be passionate about selling a particular product, but if there are no potential buyers, it will never become anything more than a hobby. The marketing plan leads you to answer this question up front. The marketing plan also forces you to think critically about what you can and can't afford. Beyond that, though, the marketing plan is simply a guess at reality. It inherently assumes that you know how a market will react to your advertising types, which no one can know for sure.

In my experience, many new business owners are married to their marketing plan. They convince themselves that how they have the business drawn up is how it will play out. This causes them to be closed off to other revenue opportunities, pricing models, and even potential customers. They put on blinders and miss opportunities to make the business expand and work.

A few years ago, I met with a business partner who had been selling some of my continuing education courses to her clients. One day, she asked if we could discuss pricing for my courses. My courses had always received positive feedback from her clients, so I thought the discussion would be around expanding our relationship. I couldn't have been more wrong.

"We need you to give us a flat rate. Your variable rate structure is killing us. Your courses are drawing too many people," she said.

Flummoxed by this demand, I asked why she felt the need for this change. She had been selling my courses since she started her business a few years ago. I hadn't raised my prices. Why the sudden demand for a different pricing structure?

She explained that, in her model, her clients paid her a flat rate, which included access to my education courses. But I asked her for a variable rate, meaning the more people who attended the class, the more money she had to pay me. My classes were drawing so many positive reviews that the word spread, and more people were coming. So many people were coming that she was actually losing money.

While I understood the numbers behind what she was saying, I struggled with the logic. Wasn't drawing more and more people to a class a good thing? People were clearly interested in my content. Wasn't this an opportunity? I decided to ask about alternatives:

"What if you price my classes differently and charge attendees a per-class fee?"

"Well, that doesn't fit our pricing model," she quickly replied.

"What if we offer some pre-recorded classes rather than live ones? It is cheaper not to have a live instructor." I was still trying to find alternatives.

"Well, we want to offer live continuing education classes only. It is part of our marketing. The only solution is for you to offer a flat rate."

This is a good example of being too married to the pricing structure and marketing plan. Neither one of us wanted to move. She was convinced that the only way to make a deal was for me to offer a flat rate. I was so convinced that a variable rate based on attendance was fair that I was not open to any other way. Each of us was missing the fact that we had a good problem: too much interest in my courses. This was an opportunity to build business and strengthen our relationship. Instead of thinking about how to capitalize on this problem, we were too busy worrying about "the hassle" of changing our marketing plans. It was silly on both sides. Once we both figured this out, we made a deal—but not without jumping through some hoops!

Whenever you put together a marketing plan, it is easy to get set in your preconceived notions about how things will come together. While starting a business with a game plan is good, the bigger matter is what happens if Plan A does not work. What does Plan B look like? What about Plan C?

In the risk management and insurance world, we often discuss scenario planning. In this exercise, you think through actionable steps you might take if certain things happen to your business. For example, how would you react if a customer lowers their prices? What happens if your website goes down? What if the price of one of your key materials increases? The goal of scenario planning is not to think of everything that could ever happen (that's not possible anyway). Instead, the point is to help the organization think through potential problems before they happen.

Scenario planning identifies vulnerabilities with the business and makes it easier to react when plans go awry. A good marketing plan should do the same thing. It should start with a base level plan, but then build in contingencies. What happens if you are not getting any traction with email marketing? What's the next move? What happens if your target market's current brand loyalty is stronger than you thought? What can you do to break this habit? By thinking through these things ahead of time, you will be more mentally and psychologically prepared to change strategic directions when (not if) things do not go quite how you think they will.

Give It Time (But Not Too Much)

Any marketer will tell you that you need to give a marketing plan a chance to develop. While there is no doubt that brand recognition takes time, you also can't wait too long to change if something is not working. For this reason, it is helpful to set guidelines ahead of time. You not only need to know what metrics will indicate success, but also when you should be hitting them.

In a previous life, I worked for a startup company that sold auto insurance policies using a website that generated quotes from several insurance carriers (think Kayak.com except with auto insurance rates). We spent a lot of time and money building a website that was user-friendly and easy to navigate. We then poured millions of dollars into TV advertising, Google advertising, and an ambitious email marketing program.

At first, our goal was simply to get people to the website, so we were happy when the number of page views trended upward. However, after a few months, we wanted more. Page views were not turning into bound insurance policies. Our marketing agencies urged us to be patient and wait for our slick new website to sink into the mighty Google algorithms and our TV jingle to become entrenched in the minds of those watching late-night TV when our commercials aired. We waited, and still nothing. We waited more, and still nothing. All the while, dollars continued to disappear.

Finally, against the wishes of our marketing agencies, we began to pull some of our expensive TV advertising and focus more on Google ads. While we were proud of our TV ads too, we wondered if someone watching TV was really compelled to jump on their laptop or phone to go and buy insurance. We also retooled the website and added articles that shared helpful insurance-buying tips. Finally, we added a button that allowed people to receive a phone call from a licensed insurance agent if they had a question and just wanted to talk to a human being. The result? We started binding policies. Sales shot up, and we had a viable business!

This is not to say that you should expect immediate success from your marketing efforts. I wish it were that simple. Most marketing efforts take time, and patience is imperative. However, don't be patient for too long, and don't be afraid to change tactics. While there are tons of good marketing agencies out there, it should be noted that many do not get paid based on your success as a business. Often, agencies will get paid regardless of their actual success. For this reason, it may be easy for them to offer "rinse and repeat" solutions when what they are doing is not working. In my experience, it is best to trust your gut and set timeframes. Switching too early may indeed cost you, but it may cost you more to wait too long.

What is a marketing channel?

Once you figure out what customers to target, you need to determine what marketing channels to use. A marketing channel is simply any method to gain attention for your product. Let's talk about a few of them.

TV Advertising

For most small businesses funded out of one's own pocket, TV advertising is not an option. It is simply too expensive. However, if you can afford it, TV is still a great way to capture many eyeballs all at once. This can be your best bet for a mainstream product aimed at the general public. TVs are in nearly every home, and many streaming services depend on ad revenue. Viewers can't easily watch TV on cable, streaming, or satellite without seeing ads. While DVRs allow for fast forwarding through ads, it is not unusual for people to still see ads while they are fast forwarding. A visually appealing ad will still generally draw attention.

That said, cost often needs to be controlled with TV. Local market advertising is generally cheaper than national advertising, so this may be an option, especially when your business is first starting. Second, the time of the day also makes a difference in price. An ad during prime time in the evening is more expensive than one at 3 a.m. on a weekday morning. Third, geography generally still matters with TV ads, too. Airing an ad in a big market (Chicago or New York) will cost more than airing an ad in a smaller market (Anderson, SC).

In general, you will purchase your ads and the station will agree to air them during the agreed-upon times. Occasionally, a station may need to bump your ad to a different time due to circumstances. For example, if a station airs a live sporting event that runs long, certain ads may not air. When this happens, a station will generally "make good" and air your ads at a different time to fill your order.

For live TV (and often streaming services, too), you'll want to evaluate the station's performance. One thing to pay attention to is not only how many of your ads aired but at what time. In general, it is more valuable to have a TV ad air during the commercial break halfway through a show rather than at the beginning or end. People may click to a different station and not see your ad if it airs between shows.

Email Marketing

Email marketing is a popular form of marketing because it is usually inexpensive and intuitive to use. Unfortunately, this can also limit its effectiveness. If everyone can utilize email marketing, then emails bombard potential customers' inboxes. Most people get hundreds of emails a day. (I counted once. I get an average of 300 emails per day!) For this medium to be effective, the question becomes: How will your emails stand out? How can you say something different amid all the noise in people's inboxes?

In the world of email marketing, there is a fine line between being helpful and being annoying. You want to be at the top of potential customers' minds for the former reason, not the latter. While answers may vary from industry to industry, I find that for many financial services professionals, anything more than two emails per week annoys the client. It should also be stated that a strong email open rate for most industries is about 20%, meaning only about one in every five emails you send will actually be read. If we send about ten emails per month (approximately two per week), only two of them will be read by our customers.

Before we get too discouraged about this, I should point out that many strategies can increase that open rate percentage. For example, the more useful an email is to the individual's situation, the more likely they are to open it. Also, if you already have an existing relationship with a client, they are more likely to open your emails. Finally, the less automated an email looks, the more likely the client is to open the email. If it arrives in the client's inbox at the same time each morning, it is very obvious that the email is automated. It is more likely that the email will be ignored. If the times are varied, the client is more likely to notice and open it.

The bottom line is that customization and individualization will increase open rates. This makes sense. Think about your own approach to your inbox in the morning. Most people go through their emails, sifting through the junk to find the emails that speak to their situation or are personalized to them. Everything else gets deleted. Our time is limited, so we only attend to the things that seem worthwhile given our situation or mindsight.

The obvious problem is that individualization and customization take time. It takes time to determine what might be on a client's mind—to figure out what they may be wrestling with and whether your product can help. Automation allows greater volumes of email to be sent, but often at the expense of customization. As a result, many companies just resign to being one email among many in the customer's inbox.

The bottom line is that email marketing may be cheap, but its effectiveness leaves much to be desired. If you can't customize emails to any significant degree, you need to make up for this inefficiency in volume (and accept the 20% open rate). To be effective, you simply need to do a lot of email marketing, which may negate some cost efficiency.

Text Messaging

In contrast to the disappointing 20% open rate for emails, the open rate on text messages is normally much higher – some sources say as high as 98%[17]. Amazingly, this statistic has remained approximately same for over 10 years[18]. Of those text messages, between 95% and 98% of them are read within minutes of receipt[19]!

This may simply point to the fact that people don't know how to delete a text message from their phone without opening it first. (As many of my friends and family members can attest, I don't!) Another explanation is that we view text messaging as a more personal form of communication. Emails and phone calls could be from anyone, but only those we are close to send us a text message.

Text messaging becomes a double-edged sword for companies. On the one hand, if you send a customer a text, it is far more likely to

17 Mackeviciute, C. (2023, August 15). *SMS Marketing Open Rates & Statistics.* Retrieved from Sender Website: https://www.sender.net/blog/sms-open-rates/

18 Johnson, D. (2011, January 30). *SMS Marketing VS Email Marketing.* Retrieved from Tatango Website: https://www.tatango.com/blog/sms-marketing-vs-email-marketing/

19 EZ Texting. (2022). *SMS Marketing Statistics.* Retrieved from EZ Texting Website: https://www.eztexting.com/sms-marketing-resources/statistics/

be opened. On the other hand, the receiver still needs to be comfortable with this form of communication. If they are not, you are more likely to be perceived as crossing a line with a text message than with a phone call or email. A text message from a business may be viewed as trespassing into one's personal space. This is especially true when a text is received after the workday is over.

This is not to say that one should never text a potential customer, but rather that caution should be used. One should step back and consider what is most comfortable to the person they are contacting. If the person you are reaching out to gave you a phone number to contact them, then clearly a phone call is best. If they circled the email address on their business card, this is a hint! Perhaps the easiest way to discern whether texting is okay is simply to ask. In my experience, most clients will tell you where the lines are if you ask them.

Legal requirements also present significant challenges for text messaging. The Telephone Consumer Protection Act (TCPA) has been around since the 1990s and has been held by the courts to apply to text messaging. Among other requirements, the TCPA limits the times when a business may text consumers to between 8 a.m. and 9 p.m. It also requires companies to keep a do-not-call/text list. Each violation of the TCPA (generally each text not in compliance with the Act) may result in a fine of up to five hundred dollars. Similarly, the CAN-SPAM Act also requires companies to allow recipients to opt out of receiving text messages. Additionally, the CAN-SPAM Act prohibits companies from reaching out to consumers with whom the company does not already have a relationship. It also prohibits a company from trying to obtain a relationship with a potential customer by texting them. All of this is to say that one should not text message clients without some forethought (and possibly a conversation with a good attorney who practices in this area).

However, even if a client has consented to text messaging and you are within the bounds of the law, context is crucial. The occasional text message may be fine. The secret to success is the ability to gauge where your clients are comfortable and read between the lines. This requires us to be perceptive, and this takes effort. Our job as marketers is to figure out where people feel most at home and connect with them that way.

Direct Mail

Direct mail marketing is a lost art form in an age where everything involves technology. However, if done correctly, a direct mail flyer or letter can get a reader's attention. People still get plenty of paper mail to their mailboxes each day, so again, the trick is trying to stand out among the stacks of bills, credit card offers, and suggestions that they may have already qualified for something.

If you already have a relationship with the customer, one way to gain attention is by offering coupons or price breaks for services. This works especially well for repeat services or products (like oil changes, baby diapers, or even certain groceries). In my experience, people like to feel like they are getting a deal—and if it is a service or product they are going to buy anyway, why not take advantage of the offer?

Establishing a relationship with a new customer is more challenging. While offering a great deal may also work for this customer, success rates are often lower. If the customer is not familiar with your product or service to begin with, what difference does a few dollars off make? It becomes even more critical to make a connection.

Handwritten letters are so rare these days that when a customer receives one, they will often read it. Letters are customizable and can be tailored to the individual client. While time-consuming, people are often struck by the fact that someone would take the time to write something only for them.

Direct mail is certainly not without its flaws. It is inefficient and slow compared to the other methods discussed. While an individualized email takes roughly the same amount of time to compose as a handwritten letter, it arrives much faster. However, direct mail is sometimes effective simply because it is different. People's inboxes are often inundated with emails, but this is probably less the case with handwritten letters. Their personalized nature and uniqueness make this marketing channel a viable strategy.

Which marketing channel is best?

There are undoubtedly other marketing channels. If you have good content, you can use your website to sell products (more on this later). You can also use a publicist to get you on TV or quoted in industry publications. You could host your podcast or try to get on other people's podcasts. All of these are possibilities. However, the main question every entrepreneur wants to know is which one is best.

The problem is that there is no one answer to this question. Certain products are more effectively sold using specific marketing channels. If you are trying to sell a new brand of snack crackers, you probably want as many eyeballs on your products as possible. Television or Internet-based (YouTube ads, Google ads, etc.) advertising may be best. The same may also be true of homeowners' or renters' insurance.

However, what if you are trying to sell banking services? Or marketing consulting services? These are services where relationships and trust are essential. Selling them the same way you would plumbing services or an energy drink may come across as insincere or deaf to the customer's needs. In these cases, you would need to build relationships with people first. You would need to attend events where potential customers might be. A banker may want to participate in a networking event for entrepreneurs or a gathering hosted by the small business association. A marketing consultant may wish to partner with accountants or financial advisors who already have relationships with potential clients. The point is that there is no one-size-fits-all when it comes to marketing channels.

When discussing the elements of a marketing plan above, I urged you to think about your buyer personas. Essentially, what are the characteristics of your target customer? Taking this a step further, what types of marketing would this target customer be most receptive to? Are there ways in which you can grab their attention more easily? Thinking about this can usually help you narrow down potential marketing channels. The marketing budget is not endless, so you want to focus on the channels that will generate the highest number of potential customers.

There is one additional piece that we need to discuss, and it is highly realistic and practical: What do you enjoy doing? When a business starts, it is often a one-person business. By default, you are doing much of your marketing. Of the effective marketing channels you can choose from, are there certain ones you would enjoy utilizing more than the others? If so, you should probably choose those! When starting a business, you don't have a reputation to lean on. You are going to have to do a lot of marketing to just gain traction. If you need to do something repeatedly, it needs to be something you enjoy (or at least can stand doing). Otherwise, you won't stick with it.

I have had a podcast for a few years now called *Accountable*. On the podcast, I talk to other people in the accounting and financial services industries about what they are doing and other hot topics. While it is a good way to bring awareness to the education events I am hosting, I also just enjoy talking with people and hearing what they are working on. I have always felt energized by these types of discussions on timely topics at CPA networking events. So, in many ways, my podcast is simply an extension of the same things I naturally do. The conversation is the same. I just hit the record button on my computer first for the podcast! It is a natural fit for me.

Many financial advisors have asked what I think about their idea for a podcast to reach potential clients. They reason that it is an easy way to tell people about their investment philosophy and discuss hot topics affecting investment portfolios. While this is not a bad idea, it only addresses one factor in the choice of marketing channel: effectiveness. My question to them is always the same: Do you enjoy talking with people and creating audio content? Can you do it over and over and over again? If the answer is yes, then a podcast could be great. If the answer is no, you should rethink this strategy. Whatever marketing channel you choose, be prepared to put some serious work into that channel. If you don't, it won't be effective. So, make it something you enjoy doing—or at least, can stand doing time and time again.

How do I get started?

Getting started marketing your product is often difficult, especially if you are not entirely sure about the proper marketing channels to reach your customers. When I started my own business, I decided to keep things as simple as possible. I knew I needed to tell people I was out on my own. I needed awareness. Therefore, I decided to tell people what I was doing through word-of-mouth. Whenever I did volunteer work, went to the grocery store, or just hung out with friends, I told people about my business. I told them what I was trying to build, who I was trying to help, and what I thought I could offer. I wouldn't spend hours on it, only a minute or two. I told them enough, but not too much.

This very simple approach helped me see other opportunities. Some people were interested in my services, others had an idea to share with me, and others would just listen and provide encouragement. In any case, I found that the more I told people about what I was doing, the more opportunities appeared. One conversation led to other conversations, and more conversations eventually led to business.

This process taught me a very valuable lesson. If you want people to know about your business, you need to tell them about it. This isn't as hard or awkward as you might initially think. After all, people talk about their work all the time. Whether catching up with an old friend or meeting someone for the first time, it is natural to ask them about their job. So why not tell them about yours? You don't need to drone on and on. You just need to answer their question when they ask what you have been up to.

The important thing is to try something. When you are first getting started, you need to gain traction. My marketing strategy was simple in the early days—just tell people what I was working on. If that doesn't work for you, try something else. The key is to try something and just start. One thing is for sure. If you do nothing, nothing will happen. That part is guaranteed!

How do you evaluate success?

Once you decide what marketing channels you will use, you need to figure out how you will gauge success. While sales numbers are an obvious choice, there are two problems with this. First, it's not always possible to connect sales back to one particular marketing channel. Second, in the early days of a business, sales may be too few and far between to give you valuable data. You may be stuck at zero sales for a while, even if you are making progress. Therefore, it may be better to start more simply than that.

When I started my business, I had no clients for about a month. Instead of focusing on sales revenue, I used earlier parts of the sales funnel to evaluate success. At first, I only looked at how many people I could talk to about my business in a day. If I could speak to at least five people, I would consider that a successful day. Later, I looked at how many people had asked about my services in a day. If at least one person inquired about me helping them, it had been a good day. Still later, I focused on how many people had signed an engagement letter. Then I finally began to focus on the number of sales and sales revenue.

When you start, it is not always possible to look at sales immediately. However, even if sales are small initially, you need to evaluate the effectiveness of your marketing. You need to figure out what is working and what isn't. What I have always told clients is to start with simple wins. If you evaluate the early parts of the marketing funnel first and take care of those, the sales will take care of themselves.

Tips for Getting to Go

1. Finding the right marketing mix takes time. Don't be afraid to try something new or take a chance.
2. Keep refining your message. Learn to tell people about your product or service in a concise way. Think about how you can address a customer's problem.
3. Use logic and take a swing. If your marketing approach misses the mark, try again and keep trying. Persistence does pay off!

CHAPTER 4

It's Not That Simple: You Need a (Secure) Website

"But aren't more visits good?" I said in a flabbergasted tone. I couldn't believe what my colleagues in the Information Technology and Data Analytics departments were telling me. I was not a technology expert, but certainly they were wrong on this one, right?

"Those aren't real people. Those are most likely bots," she said in a monotone voice. She was a friend of mine, and she could tell this was blowing my mind. Her patience was appreciated.

"Are you sure? How can you tell?" I said, still in disbelief.

"There are ways," she said. "It doesn't mean we're not doing well. It just means the number of website visitors probably isn't as high as it looks. The data is still valuable."

I have never been a technology person. I have never been enamored with the latest and greatest software. I still haven't fallen in love with AI. I have plenty of friends who are this way. They give me strange looks when I admit how little I know. What's funny is that I deeply respect technology even though I know little about it. I know that it is hard to run a business without embracing technology to some degree. Perhaps that's why I always tell even the smallest business that they need a website, and it must be secure.

My reasoning is based on how people search for and buy products. What is the first thing you do when seeking out a particular product or service? You Google it. What is the first thing you do when meeting someone for the first time? You look for them on social media. It has become so commonplace that it feels strange to us in situations where we can't do it. Right after I bought my home in rural Ohio, I remember becoming frustrated at my inability to find a local home cleaning service. I tried every Google search I could. I looked on Facebook, LinkedIn, and every social media platform I could think of. By the time I was ready to give up, I saw a flyer at a local laundromat. It turns out there were several options, but none of them were online. I remember being shocked that I had to call each one individually! My brain couldn't get over the idea that someone *wouldn't* be on social media.

Let me be clear. There are lots of problems with social media and technology. Over the last few years, we have learned that there are downsides to being online: Isolation, depression, and self-esteem issues come to mind. However, we need to admit to ourselves that having a website is also mandatory these days—especially post-pandemic, when many people are working from home. They can't see your physical storefront if they don't leave the house. Your homepage is your new storefront. Without it, in many potential customers' eyes, you don't exist.

Do I really need a website?

Yes. Until you have a storefront, you can't sell anything. Until you sell something, you can't make money. In this day and age, it is expected to have a website. When you don't have one, people wonder if you are legitimate. For this reason, one-person companies need a website just as badly (if not more so) than established companies. When you are first starting out, you are often fighting for credibility. Potential customers may not trust you yet because they are not familiar with your product or service. You work harder for sales because your reputation cannot carry you yet. In the early days, especially, you don't want to do anything to hurt your ability to make sales. Having a website is most likely not going to hurt your reputation. In many cases, it can only help.

If you don't know how to build a website, you have choices. One option is to hire someone to do it for you. Just like any other part of your business that you choose to outsource, there is a risk that comes with this option. The quality and effectiveness of the web design may be challenging to judge upfront. Also, this can be pretty expensive depending on who you hire and the scope of what you want built. Coders and web developers are in high demand, so the good ones tend to be costly and may be difficult to schedule.

Another option is to do some of the work yourself. In many cases, website-building platforms offer design templates. The user then selects a template and customizes it to their needs. While this may not provide all of the features a coder could design for you, it at least gives you something. It creates a web presence and is much better than having nothing.

There are other options between these two. As I have always told clients, everything in business is a cost-benefit decision. You need to figure out if the dollars you spend on an outside developer are worth the time saved from you doing something yourself. Also, you should think about upkeep. Once the website's initial design is done, you need to think about how you will maintain it. Do you want to update the content yourself or have someone else do it? What happens if you need to make changes to how clients contact you? What happens if your product offerings change? Who updates your website? Is it you? Or someone else? If you choose to outsource this function, it may be best to get the person who designed the site to be the one who keeps it up.

Where do I even start?

Even if you decide to outsource your website build, it is crucial to think through what you want your website to do. More specifically, what do you want the people who visit your website to do? If you are a contractor, you may want people visiting your website to contact you about potential jobs. If you are selling a product, you may want them to purchase the product directly from your website. If you are an accountant, you may want visitors to learn about what you offer and make an appointment to discuss their specific needs. The point is to consider the website's goal; how does it fit into your overall business strategy? Website developers are going to ask you this. So even if you outsource, you must figure out what you want.

Once you identify your goal for the website, you can think about design, which should cater to that goal. If your goal is to build client relationships through your website, you might add blog posts about common problems a client might have and how you can help. If your goal is to get people to purchase your product directly from your website, tell them why your product is something they need.

You can add many bells and whistles to a website, but ultimately, these technologically advanced features only matter if your website serves your business needs. Focus more on making sure that the website meets your overall goal. If certain features or types of content meet this goal, then you should use them. If not, then save yourself the money and time involved in adding them.

How do I direct users on my website?

If you want a website that meets your goals, you need to make it easy for visitors. If people have to search for the purchase button or cannot easily locate how to contact you, your website is not serving its purpose. This is a failure. Whatever you want them to do, make it easy for them. This will increase your chances for success.

When I worked for a startup auto insurance company, we decided that the primary purpose of our website was to drive quotes. We wanted website visitors to enter enough information into our website so that we could give them a rate. While not everyone would actually bind an insurance policy with us, purchase only became possible after a quote. The more quotes we received, the more purchases would be made. As a result, we tried several options for where to place the quote button on our website. After several different attempts with varying degrees of success, we decided to have the quote button on every page. That way, no matter where someone entered the website, they would have the opportunity to quote. We tried to make it so the quote button was not too "in their face" (there is such a thing as being too aggressive even on a website), but also easily accessible. Through trial and error, we eventually came to a satisfactory solution.

One tip to remember when thinking through these concepts for your products and services is that people don't scroll. This sounds strange, but think about how you view websites. Unless there is a reason to scroll down (a story you want to read, etc.), you typically only look at what immediately appears on the page. A paper newspaper has to be folded in half. People thinking about purchasing the newspaper that day would generally only browse the stories at the top of the first page—the stories "above the fold." The same is true of websites. People typically only view the things immediately on the first page. If you want someone to do something, you should place that button or object above the fold. If the consumer has to scroll, you generally will not see nearly as many hits.

Can driving phone calls be my website's goal?

I have never been a fan of websites that are just "glorified business cards." Many service-based businesses do this, like accounting firms, financial advisors, and others with tailored product offerings. While it is understandable not to want to offer a quote online, this does the customer a disservice. A customer may be seeking you out online because they don't want to call you yet. They are trying to learn about you before determining if a phone call is warranted. By simply having a website that tells them to call you, you may actually turn them off.

The other problem with the website-as-business-card approach is that many service-based websites forget to tell clients what services they actually offer. For example, an accounting firm that simply says that it offers "tax services" doesn't answer the question of whether it can do the bookkeeping for my small business. This lack of clarity also does a disservice to a potential client trying to find answers as quickly as possible.

If the goal of your website really is to get customers to call you, you still need to say something about your product or service on the website. Tell the customer something they did not know before. Tell them about your process and what makes you different. If you can't give them an exact price, tell them a range. If you specialize in a particular type of client situation, tell them that. People seek out websites to learn something about the company. When they come away learning nothing, it can leave a bad taste in their mouth—even if the product is precisely what they are looking for. If you can tell them something they did not know before, you provide value and make it more likely that they will call.

SEO sounds like a disease—do I need to catch it?

When people search for something online, most only look at the first few search results. It is rare for someone to flip over to the second page of results. For this reason, it is vital to have your page near the top. Search engine optimization (SEO) refers to the techniques companies use to ensure they appear at the top of the search results. SEO is something that every business owner needs to deal with. There are various ways to do this, but specialists will often utilize a few key tools:

- **Content Optimization & Links/Backlinks**: Search engines will seek out high-quality content on your website that is easy to navigate and find. Links to your website, as well as links to other websites with relevant content, can also help drive traffic to your landing pages.

- **Technical & Algorithm Requirements**: Search engines use certain algorithms and technical requirements that must be met before your website appears in a search. An SEO specialist can help you navigate these rules.
- **Keyword Searches**: An SEO specialist can also help you define what keyword searches your website should show up for.

SEO is not something that can be perfected overnight. It is important but also requires specialized knowledge. It takes a long time to show up as the top search result. You may also need to pay for preferred positioning on the search page over your competitors.

For a new business, SEO is probably not the number one priority. The higher priority is having a website that is useful when people visit. Still, if you plan on growing a business consistently over time, it is best to look at SEO sooner rather than later. If you do, it will be there for you when you need it.

How do I market my business in a highly regulated industry?

Working in financial services most of my career, I can identify with this sentiment. In specific industries, you cannot say certain things because it is deemed misleading or harmful to the public. You should always make sure you know the regulatory requirements for your industry, and you should always make sure your website is compliant. Nothing will kill a good idea faster than falling out of compliance. But within the rules for your industry, what *can* you say that will help meet customers' needs? What do you want customers to do? The key is to answer their questions while staying within what the rules allow.

You should also consider the security you need on your website. Customer data, payment information, and other details about your clients need to stay private. For this reason, you need to consider the security your website provider gives you. If you need outside help, engaging a website specialist may be the way to go. You should also look at obtaining cyber liability insurance (more on this in the next chapter). The bottom line is that you have a responsibility as a company to keep data private. If you don't, you may need to pay federal *and* state penalties imposed by regulators. Cyber criminals continue to get smarter. It is wise to invest in this area early so your business's reputation can continue to grow.

While regulations provide a challenge, none should keep a company from presenting a website that is helpful to clients, and they are certainly no excuse for omitting a website altogether. You still need one in almost any business—you just need to be responsible when you create one.

How do I know if the website is working?

Evaluating website effectiveness has become easier with more off-the-shelf software products, like Google Analytics, becoming available. As we discussed in the marketing chapter, it is important to keep perspective on how you measure success. That said, even the smallest of small business owners can glean some information about what is or is not working on their website.

When I went out on my own, I built my company's first website using a templated resource I found online. Very few people knew the website existed initially, so sales were not a viable metric. At first, I started by just evaluating page views. I considered what I could do to drive traffic. I spent what little money I had on SEO and began to look more specifically at what pages my visitors were looking at. Only over time could we start evaluating success beyond just simple website visitors.

As my colleague pointed out in the opening vignette to this chapter, it is helpful to remember that website data may not be perfect initially. This can be for several reasons (as I found out as a young CFO, one of those reasons can be bots visiting the website). Therefore, it is probably best to focus on the trajectory of the data in the early days of a business, rather than the actual numbers themselves. If you are getting more website visits, clicks, and purchases, you are probably headed in the right direction.

If you are not getting the desired results, dig in to understand why. Are there pages where people are dropping off? Are there particular parts of your website that are difficult to navigate? Does your website load too slowly? I realize this can be a frustrating process of guess-and-check. However, in many cases, you can discern the problem spots by putting yourself in your client's shoes.

Tips for Getting to Go

1. Websites need to evolve as your business does. Periodically, you should consider whether your website needs an upgrade. Like any other part of your marketing mix, your website cannot get stale. If it does, it starts to become less effective.
2. Ask people for feedback on your website. Ask existing clients, potential clients, friends, and family. Try to get some perspective on your website from a variety of sources. Don't just rely on your observations or your employees' observations. You may be "too close" to make truly unbiased observations.

3. Remember that websites are often your storefront these days. What yours says about you is important—especially in the early days when you are working to get clients to notice you!

CHAPTER 5

It Can Be Worse: You Need Insurance

I was sick a lot as a kid. I had allergies and asthma, along with many prescribed medications to help me feel better. The only problem is that the medicine tasted awful, so I would try to avoid taking it at all costs. My mother, a former nurse, tried every trick in the book to get me to take my medicine. She put it in apple sauce. She put it in drinks. A few times, she even told me it was something else, hoping she could trick me into eating it. However, I quickly picked up when something was amiss and could usually spit out whatever it was in the nick of time. It just tasted awful. So, I concluded the only thing that made sense to my young mind: I would just stay sick forever. After all, anything had to be better than that garbage the doctor was trying to force down my gullet!

One day, my mother had all but given up on trying to get me to drink some nasty elixir. She had tried everything else, so she decided to just level with me. She said, "David, I know this stuff tastes awful. But I don't want to see you get sick, so you need to drink it.

This is bad, but isn't not being able to go outside and play with your friends worse?"

What kind of mind control was this? She had me feeling bad and finding it difficult to carry on my staunch resistance against the doctors, caring parents, and modern medicine. I had no choice. I choked down the supposedly cherry-flavored liquid, made a face, and then went into the other room to watch cartoons on TV, feeling bewildered over what just happened.

Whenever I tell a new business owner they need to consider getting insurance, I often think their reaction is similar to that of me in early grade school. It's not like they don't know what insurance is or why it is important. However, money is tight, and the last thing they want to do is choke down another cost. They also think they are so small that nothing can happen to them. This piece of advice has a bitter taste, but if you don't get it, the possible outcomes are much worse.

Do I have to buy insurance?

Most new business owners do not argue with the logic of having insurance. They know it is the right thing to do and that all businesses have insurance. Instead, many new business owners argue about timing. They will say things like, "I just want to wait until I get a bit bigger and have the money to pay for it." The problem with this logic is that the early stages of the business are when the business is most vulnerable to claims. Think about it. When do mistakes most often happen? When the business is young and the processes aren't down to a science quite yet. When are we most likely to take on jobs and clients that we shouldn't? When the business is first starting, we often try to sell our product to anyone; our vetting process is not mature enough for us to find that ideal client. When do we know the least about our business and the industry that we are in? When the business is first starting, no matter how long we have worked in an industry, it is tough to know everything. We just don't know what we don't know. Our business is most vulnerable to a possible claim when it is first starting. Therefore, we need to buy insurance right at the beginning of our business's life.

I know what you are thinking. Dave is an insurance guy. He has a background in insurance, so of course, he will say I need insurance right away. My background notwithstanding, the problem is that nothing can kill momentum faster than an insurance claim. If you get sued for something early on, you may not have the financial backing to come back from it. Your dream may die before the public has even had a chance to see it. That's just sad!

I am not advocating that you buy every insurance policy imaginable immediately so you can become bulletproof. First, that's impossible (even if you have insurance, you can still end of paying for mistakes). Of course, we also need to make cost-benefit decisions (it is business after all). But what you do need is to take a hard look at the risks your company faces and figure out how to address them. To do this, you need to understand something about risk management and where insurance fits into this framework.

How do risk management and insurance fit together?

Insurance can't cover every single risk that a business faces. For example, every business faces the risk that the economy will take a bad turn and profits will deteriorate. No company is completely immune to the world economy. It isn't possible to cover this risk with insurance. A second example might involve competitors. There is a risk that your company's competitors could lower their prices, causing you to lose customers. Again, no insurance policy covers this risk. For this reason, insurance is one part of the risk management framework. It is one tool for managing risk, not the only way to manage risk. How do we know what risks we need to manage? Identifying them is the first step in the risk management process.

Step 1: Identify Risks

There are many ways to identify the risks a company faces. Some industries have standardized checklists online. For example, the US Department of Agriculture has a standardized checklist for farmers to assess their risks. The Risk Management Society (RIMS) also has several checklists available. However, when you have a brand new idea or are trying something that breaks ground in a new industry, finding a standardized checklist may be unrealistic. In this case, it may be more helpful to think about what would kill your business model. What could go wrong that would be the most damaging to your business? If there are businesses similar to yours in your chosen industry already, what are the most perilous problems they face?

I encountered this question of risk when I worked for a start-up company that was a price comparison website for auto insurance rates. While the idea of price comparison for insurance was widely accepted in the United Kingdom and throughout Europe, it was a new concept in the United States. We didn't have any true competitors yet. While we could use our European counterparts as a starting point, the insurance markets were vastly different between the United States and Europe. In many ways, when trying to figure out what risks we faced as a company, we were starting from a blank slate.

When putting together our first risk register, I remember throwing my hands up and scribbling down all the ideas of what could happen to us. Since we anticipated that nearly all our sales would be through the Internet, the prospect of our website going down would be catastrophic. We decided early on that was our most threatening risk. Since visitors coming to our website were entering personal information, another significant risk was that the data could be stolen if we did not safeguard it well enough. Another major risk was related to the proprietary design of the website. We had to protect against the possibility that one of our website developers would resign from our company to join a new firm. Slowly, our risk register was born.

The bottom line is that sometimes the easiest way to identify the risks that your new business will face is to take a quiet moment to think about it. As a friend of mine would say, logic your way through it. One thing to remember is that risk identification is iterative, meaning you are constantly doing it. You don't just identify risks once. You continually track new risks as the company changes and evolves. The key is to identify the most critical risks now so you can do something about them. You can worry about the rest next time.

Step 2: Assess the Risks

Not every risk you identify is going to be an equal threat. Some risks will have more damage potential than others. To figure out which risks are the most threatening, risk management professionals will often score risks in terms of frequency and severity. The frequency of a risk is how often it is likely to happen. More frequent risks are scored higher than risks that risks that are rare. Severity refers to the ensuing damage if the risk were to materialize. This is measured by dollars, which could mean lost business, equipment replacement costs, or damages. Risks are then plotted based on this scoring. For example, if we used a 1 to 5 scoring matrix for frequency and severity, it might look something like this:

SEVERITY					
5	M	H	H	H	H
4	M	M	H	H	H
3	L	L	M	M	H
2	L	L	L	L	M
1	L	L	L	L	L
	1	2	3	4	5

FREQUENCY

RED GREEN YELLOW

While we can disregard the risks in the green quadrants, we should be most concerned with the ones in the red. These are the ones we must get a handle on right at the outset. You won't be able to handle everything immediately and not every potential incident is going to blow up the business. However, whether you do this scoring formally or informally, you should prioritize which risks you need to handle right away. My advice is always to deal with the big items first.

Step 3: Consider Controls

Once you have a list of risks and have prioritized them through scoring, you need to evaluate what mitigating factors are already in place and which you still must implement in order to cut down on the damaging effects of each major risk. Risk controls can generally be broken down into the following categories:

- **Avoidance**: One way to ensure you don't have any problems with any risks identified in your risk register is to avoid them altogether. For example, if one risk you identified is the possibility of flooding at your office because it is next to a body of water, you could move offices. This would certainly eliminate that possibility. However, while avoidance is very effective, it is often impractical. Let's say you are working as a construction contractor and the risk you face is getting sued due to poor workmanship. The most effective solution would be to simply not do any construction work! That would seem to create problems with the business plan, though, wouldn't it? Hence, there are other ways to control risks if avoidance isn't practical.

- **Loss Prevention**: Another way to control risks is by introducing measures to prevent losses. An example might be completing safety training or certifying yourself (or implementing mandatory safety training for your employees). This training might not reduce the dollar cost when an accident happens (severity), but it would presumably reduce the number of accidents (frequency).
- **Loss Reduction**: While loss prevention focuses on reducing the number of accidents or claims, loss reduction focuses on reducing the dollar amounts of a claim. A good example of this might be installing sprinklers in a building. The sprinklers do not reduce the frequency of fires occurring in a building, but they do reduce the amount of damage inflicted.
- **Separation**: As the name implies, this risk control technique involves separating risks, so that if one item is affected, it does not affect all items. A good example would be where a retail store keeps some items in one warehouse and others in a different warehouse. If a loss were to occur on one of the warehouses, damaging the inventory inside, the company would still have at least some of its inventory in another location.
- **Duplication**: Duplication involves keeping multiple copies of certain items. For example, a company might have its files backed up on a cloud-based server each night. If the primary server were to be damaged or corrupted, the files could be retrieved through the backup server. The biggest problem with duplication is the cost involved. In a sense, duplication involves

buying two items where only one is required. In the example above, two servers would be needed even though the company only needs one to function.

- **Diversification**: Diversification is often used in the investment world to describe the technique of combining certain risks so that they offset each other and, therefore, reduce the overall risk the company faces. For example, a company might offer multiple products to the public. If one product does not sell, the company might still be able to make money on the other one.

You might use one or several of these techniques, depending on your business model and industry. The point is to ascertain what controls you already have in place—or which ones you can easily implement—and how these mitigate the risk. Does this change the scoring or prioritization of your risks? If so, which are now the major risks that you need to deal with?

Step 4: Implement Risk Financing Techniques

For risks that remain, we need to consider risk financing techniques. Risk financing techniques generally fall into two buckets:

- **Risk Transfer**: This involves transferring the responsibility for paying the damages caused by a loss event to another person or entity. Insurance is one form of risk transfer, but it is certainly not the only one. A hold harmless agreement that basically makes another company or a client liable for damages would be another form of risk transfer. Risk transfer techniques don't reduce the possibility that a claim might happen; they simply push the responsibility for paying for that loss over to another entity or person.

- **Risk Retention**: As stated earlier, insurance may not cover everything. Therefore, when insurance cannot cover something, the company has no choice but to pay for losses as they happen. You may proactively choose to retain the risk because you don't want to pay for the insurance. It should be noted that risk retention is also the default choice if you don't identify a potential risk. If you don't know a loss exposure exists and then the loss happens, you must pay for it. In a sense, by not doing anything about a risk, you retain it—whether you want to or not.

Step 5: Monitor the Risks

Once you have done everything you can to address your company's risks, you should continue to monitor new risks that may emerge. You will address risks as they come up. In this way, the risk management process is never done. You are always evaluating new potential losses and risks as the company changes, customers' tastes and preferences evolve, or the industry adapts to a changing world. Keep your eyes peeled and pay attention to what is happening around you.

For those who tend to have perfectionistic tendencies (as a tax accountant by trade, I would raise my hand here!), it is now time to tell you something you don't want to hear: You won't be able to think of everything your new business will face ahead of time (do you hear that bubble bursting?). We are all limited by what we can think of in the moment we are in. I am confident that most companies did not have a contingency plan for COVID-19 when it happened. After all, who could foresee a global pandemic? In many ways, when a business starts, you are limited by your imagination.

When I started my current company, I had to fine-tune our client engagement letter multiple times before I got it right. I wrote a first draft, but I realized quickly that clients were having trouble locating my fees within the engagement letter (even when I pointed out what page they could be found on in an accompanying email). I pivoted to put my fees up at the top of the engagement letter in bold on the first page. Several prospects struggled to understand that certain services required a different engagement letter. Therefore, I changed the engagement letter again, so that the services *not* included were in a more clearly labeled list. The point here is that risk management is never done. As you learn things about your business, clients, and yourself, you will discover more risks that need to be addressed.

If you take nothing else from these steps in the risk management process, please note one thing: understanding the major risks your business faces can save you time, headaches, and money. You can adjust your business model in ways that streamline it. You can avoid unnecessary insurance costs as well. Insurance companies know that claims can be much worse if you don't take the time to implement controls. If you do what you can to mitigate risks outside of insurance, your premiums will be lower on the insurance policies you must pay for.

What can be covered with insurance?

Insurance addresses low-frequency, high-severity loss exposures. In other words, insurance works well to address losses that don't happen often, but when they do, they cost the company a lot of money. Before talking to an insurance broker, you should have an idea of which risks you would like to retain and which need to be covered. This will make your conversation more productive and focused.

In general, a good insurance program for a company will start with a foundational package policy. Specialty policies may then be added to address risks unique to your industry. Finally, an umbrella (or excess loss policy) will be added as an extra layer of protection against catastrophic claims. It may be helpful to think of the insurance program in layers.

Umbrella Policy
Specialty Policies
Package Policy

Since one usually puts the package policy in place first, let's start there.

Package Policies

There are two basic types of package policies: business owners policy (BOP) and commercial package policy (CPP). Both a BOP and a CPP are made up of multiple coverages that most businesses need. For example, coverages might include:

- Commercial Property
- Business Income & Extra Expenses Coverage
- Commercial Inland Marine
- Computer Systems Coverage
- Equipment Breakdown Coverage
- Cause of Loss Special Form
- Personal Property Coverage
- Commercial Crime Coverage
- Annual Transit Coverage
- Contractors Equipment Coverage
- Commercial General Liability Coverage
- Business Auto Coverage

The big difference between a BOP and a CPP is how they are underwritten. When an insurance company quotes a company for a BOP policy, it will use simplified underwriting. BOPs are specifically made for smaller companies, so the insurance company will essentially quote the policy based on a limited number of questions. When the company is larger and needs a CPP, the insurance company understandably wants to get a better idea of the risks that the company faces. Therefore, more questions will be asked on the application, and a site visit may be necessary.

It should be noted that there is no standard situation where an insurance company must underwrite a BOP versus a CPP. Companies utilize their own criteria to delineate when one should be used over another. For example, an insurer might say that a company qualifies for a BOP if it meets all of the following criteria:

- Has fewer than fifty employees
- One location, office, or premises
- Less than $750,000 in annual revenue, based on the last three years (or projected)
- No revenue increases of over 20% in the past year
- Operates in a low-risk industry and has not been acquired (or party to a merger)
- Less than twelve months of business income insurance needed

By meeting these criteria, the company can get a cheaper premium rate than it could with a CPP, and the insurance company saves time by not having to send a representative to evaluate the risks more closely.

Since insurance companies often have unique criteria for underwriting a BOP, engaging with an insurance broker is helpful. While you will need to pay an insurance broker a commission if you purchase a policy, they can reach out to commercial insurance companies on your behalf and help you get the best rates.[20]

Specialty Policies

Remember that the package policy provides the coverages that most businesses need. It does not account for the unique aspects of your work. In short, you may need additional coverage in certain areas simply because of the nature of your business. This is where specialty policies come in.

Imagine you are operating an online store that collects customer and credit card information to process sales. Compared to the average company, you have a much greater exposure to customer data being compromised via unauthorized access to your website. In this instance, you would likely need a cyber liability policy in addition to your package policy. Similarly, a taxicab company would likely need more commercial auto insurance coverage than the average company, considering the number of cars in their fleet and the amount of driving they do. In each of these instances, the unique aspects of the business create a need for specialized coverages beyond the package policy.

Umbrella Policies

While many business owners just getting started are tempted to skip the umbrella coverage, this is often a mistake. Umbrella policies

20 I am normally not a fan of paying for things you can do yourself. As a small business owner, you should save money where possible. However, unless you work in commercial insurance, you will probably not be able to do the legwork to find a good insurance policy yourself. It is time-consuming, and that time may be better spent dealing with the other facets of getting your business off the ground. If you decide to try it yourself, be prepared to spend hours digging into the details of the policies.

cover losses that exceed the coverage amounts in your package and specialty policies. Let's say you have $100,000 of coverage for a claim in a package policy. If you had a claim totaling $250,000, the insurance company would only be responsible for the first $100,000 of that claim. The remaining $150,000 would come out of your pocket. This is where an umbrella policy can help. An umbrella policy would cover the amounts over and above the underlying policy coverages (package and specialty coverages).

A few things should be mentioned here. First, umbrella policies generally require you to maintain the underlying coverages. Changes in your package or specialty policies must be reported to the insurance company that wrote your umbrella policy. If they are not, you would likely be responsible for the claim that your underlying policies would have covered had they been in place.

Second, the premium on an umbrella policy is usually much cheaper than for the package or specialty policy coverages. To understand this, it is helpful to have a basic understanding of how insurance companies price their policies. In general, the premium you pay is made up of three primary components:

Average cost of claims for that policy type + Insurance company administrative costs + Insurance company profit margin = Premium you pay[21]

Since the umbrella policy will only pay for claims that exceed the underlying policy limits, this means that very few claims will actually be paid by the umbrella insurance company. Most claims will be paid by the underlying policies. Since the average claims cost is lower for the umbrella insurance provider, the premium is generally much cheaper for the coverage you get.

---

21 Please note that this formula is greatly simplified. In real life, insurance companies incorporate more factors and certain underwriting criteria. However, for our purposes, this formula illustrates the concept well.

My grandmother used to say, "Nothing is a big deal until it is." I think this is especially true in the case of umbrella insurance. Most people don't really think too much about catastrophic claims until they have one. Umbrella insurance is a cost-efficient way to avoid the impact of a large claim early in a company's life.

Finding Information in the Insurance Policy

Once the insurance policies are written and the company has them in place, you should have an idea of what is covered and what isn't. In short, you should read the policy!

In my experience, most people don't have a problem with this concept. However, the amount of information contained in a commercial insurance policy can be overwhelming. For this reason, it is helpful to know a bit about how policies are organized.

Parts of the Standard Property & Casualty Insurance Policy

Since property and casualty insurance policies are often regulated and standardized, there are common elements you will see in nearly every policy:

- **Declarations**: The declarations page is often a short (usually only a page or two) summary of the major components of the coverages located near the front of the policy. It will show the insured's name, coverage limits, location of property covered by the policy, dates the policy is in force, and other common details. A bank, mortgage lender, or business partner may request a declarations page to show proof of insurance.

- **Insuring Agreements**: At its heart, an insurance policy is a contract between you and the insurance company. Like any other contract, promises are made on both sides. You promise to pay the policy premium. In exchange, the insurance company promises to pay covered claims, as long as you meet the conditions outlined in the policy.
- **Definitions**: Like many other industries, insurance has its own language. The definitions page describes what key terms in the policy mean. It also describes who is being referred to when the policy says "we" or "you."
- **Conditions**: For an insurance company to pay a claim, the insured is often required to act in a way that will not make the claim worse (and allow the insurance company to examine the damages quickly). For example, an insurance company may require that a police report be filed for a claim or that you make reasonable efforts to protect assets to avoid further damage.
- **Exclusions**: An insurance company generally will not cover certain acts or property for the following reasons: a) the item or act is better covered under a different type of policy, b) the event is not an accident, or c) the item is too difficult to cover. In any case, reviewing the exclusions section of any policy is important. The financial responsibility for anything that is excluded under the policy remains with you!
- **Miscellaneous Provisions**: This part is a catch-all section that might describe things like how the policy may be cancelled or other administrative details.

When looking through each of these sections, it is important to remember a few things:

- **Wear-and-tear is *never* covered.** Insurance covers accidents, not damage from regular use over time. Equipment must be replaced every so often. This is not an insurance matter; it just needs to be budgeted for.
- **Foreseeable events or acts are *never* covered.** Insurance is not meant to cover situations where the damage is a likely outcome of a conscious act. If you act recklessly, the insurance company may not pay a claim, since you should have been able to see that a problem might ensue. This is especially important to remember during holiday party time before deciding to serve alcohol.
- **Not all exclusions apply to all parts of the policy.** When reviewing something like a package policy where several coverages are rolled up under one, it is important to remember that exclusions may apply to one section, several sections, or the entire policy. It is important to know what part of the policy you are looking at, so that you can make this distinction.
- **Deductibles are really a form of retention.** In many cases, coverages will have a deductible associated with them. You must pay this amount before the insurance company will reimburse a claim. For example, let's say you had a claim totaling $1,500. If your policy only had a deductible of $500, then you would pay the first $500 of that claim, and the insurance company would pay the remaining $1,000. However, if the claim were only $485, you would be responsible for paying the entire amount, since it was under your $500 deductible.

It is important to pay attention to deductibles in the insurance policy since this represents the amount that you are still responsible for if a claim occurs. A higher deductible will normally result in a lower premium owed. It will cost you less money to obtain the policy, but you may have to pay more out of pocket to cover losses. Lower deductibles will generally result in the insurance company reimbursing a higher percentage of the claim, but you pay more up front in the form of the policy premium.

How much insurance do I need?

This is the magic question! Many factors go into this, but essentially, you want to have enough coverage to pay for any claims that may arise. For example, if you are covering your business property, you would want to cover the full value of the property. A building that is worth one million should have one million in property coverage. The same would hold true for the business equipment you own.

Insurance companies typically incentivize customers to insure property to value—that is, for how much the property is actually worth. They do this by using something called a coinsurance clause. A coinsurance clause basically says that for the entire claims cost to be covered, the insurance policy must cover a certain percentage of the property's value when the claim happens. For example, let's say the insurance on your building has a 90% coinsurance clause. If your building had a value of $500,000 at the time of the claim, you would need at least $450,000 worth of coverage ($500,000 x 90% = $450,000) for the entire claim to be covered. If you don't have coverage in at least that amount, your insurance company will cover part of the claim cost, but not all of it. You won't get your full reimbursement. For this reason, it is prudent to review policies each year to ensure that the value shown in the policy keeps up with the actual value of the property. This can be difficult for some items, like real estate, which tend to appreciate in value over time.

For liability coverage, you would want to cover the damages you might cause. Insurance brokers can be helpful in estimating coverage needs because they see lots of claims every day for businesses that are probably similar to yours. However, if you ever find yourself in a situation where you need to estimate this amount yourself, my best advice is always to guess high. There are usually more components to a claim than you might expect.

Let's say you accidentally run into a client's car when leaving their parking lot. In addition to paying for the replacement parts on the other vehicle, you will need to pay for the cost of labor, as well as any towing costs. Depending on the amount of damage, the client may need a rental car for some time, too, while their car gets fixed. The point is that the actual cost of a claim may be more than what initially meets the eye, meaning you need more coverage.

A Primer on Business Insurance

If you are new to the world of business insurance, it is helpful to know what some of the standard coverage types are. Remember that a package policy may give basic protection for each of these coverages, but you may need a specialty policy if the basic coverage is not enough for your particular business.

Professional Liability Coverage

Professional liability insurance covers your negligent acts when you are working within your chosen profession. It is also sometimes called errors and omissions coverage, depending on your profession. Doctors, dentists, attorneys, accountants, insurance agents, and many other professionals need professional liability coverage in order to do their work. For example, if a tax accountant makes a mistake on a tax return and gets sued by a client, this claim would be covered under a professional liability insurance policy. It covers negligent acts, but only when the act is within the scope of your profession.

Commercial General Liability Coverage

In contrast to professional liability insurance (which covers negligence in your professional acts), commercial general liability insurance (CGL) covers nonprofessional negligent acts. What's the difference? Continuing from the example above, let's say someone slips and falls while walking into their accountant's office. This claim would not be covered under the accountant's professional liability policy. That only covers professional acts, like the accountant preparing tax returns or giving tax advice. Assuming that the accountant was liable for the person falling (maybe they were so excited to get to the office that they did not clear all the ice from the sidewalk), the claim would be under the accountant's CGL policy. There are three different parts to the standard CGL policy:

- **Part A—Bodily Injury & Property Damage:** covers you or your employees for injuries you cause to others or property.
- **Part B—Personal & Advertising Injury:** covers instances where you or your employees are sued for libel, slander, false arrest, copyright infringement, or malicious prosecution.
- **Part C—Medical Payments:** covers reasonable costs for medical treatment, hospital expenses, ambulance costs, and funeral expenses of customers, business partners, and other non-employees. (Employee medical costs would generally be covered under a workers' compensation plan or the employee's health insurance.)

It is not unusual for business partners to insist that the companies with which they work have CGL coverage. When estimating how much coverage is needed, you generally want to consider the largest claim possible (not just the minimum requested coverage from the business partner).

Buildings & Personal Property Insurance (BPP)

Even if you have a service-based business, you will probably need at least some equipment or other business property in order to operate. For example, even someone like a business consultant will probably need at least a laptop and a cellphone to communicate with clients. Coverage for the business property you own, as well as any buildings that you own, is under a BPP policy. In addition to covering your property, a BPP also covers any property that is in your possession that belongs to others. This could be property you are leasing, inventory you have on premises, or even your interest in any improvements made on the property. As stated earlier, you want to insure your property to its full value.

It is not unusual these days to work from home on a regular basis. You may not even have a physical office. However, even in these situations, it is important to obtain coverage under a separate commercial property policy. Standard homeowners' insurance policies provide very little coverage for property that is damaged while being used for business purposes. This is also true of the standard renter's policy as well. To make sure you are covered for any claims that happen while you are working, you should have a separate business policy.

Cyber & Privacy Insurance Policies

Perhaps the most common additional coverage that most businesses need is a cyber insurance policy. If you are involved in selling your product (or even if you are just collecting information) over the Internet, you will more than likely need a cyber insurance policy. This will give you protection in the case where website visitors' or customers' information is leaked or in the case where your systems are compromised by malware.

It is important to realize that if people's personal information is leaked due to your systems, you may have broken the law. You may be fined by regulators or sued. For those whose information was compromised, you may have to pay for notification costs and credit monitoring. These costs can be very high, and in extreme cases, can put you out of business. Here are common situations that are often covered in cyber policies:

- Notification Costs
- Credit Monitoring
- Costs to Defend Regulator Claims
- Fines and Penalties
- Loss Resulting from Identity Theft
- File Recovery Costs
- Investigation Costs
- Data stored on laptops and other portables
- Information stored on the cloud
- Information stored both offline and online
- Advertising and other content
- Crisis management and PR costs
- Cyber extortion

The cost of cyber policies can vary greatly. In general, the more information you keep about customers (or potential customers), the steeper the price. Also, the *type* of information you keep matters as well. For example, if you keep information like Social Security Numbers or credit card information, your cyber policy will be more expensive than if you are just storing customer responses about your product. The more sensitive the information, the more the policy costs (because the bigger the cost would be if that information were compromised).

It is important to realize that not everyone's cyber insurance needs are the same. If your business is highly dependent on Internet sales, then your cyber insurance needs are much higher than if you only use the Internet to tell the world your name, hours of operation, and phone number. In today's world, though, it is extremely rare to have a company that genuinely does not do anything over the Internet. Therefore, you should almost always consider obtaining a cyber policy early on in your company's life.

Take a Step Back

Whenever I talk to business owners about insurance, it is easy for them to get caught up in everything that can go wrong. It is understandable to feel intimidated and overwhelmed. I am not trying to say that everything that *can* go wrong *will* go wrong with your business. Nor am I trying to say that you should buy every insurance policy out there. You don't need coverage for everything. And like anything else in business, you need to weigh the peace of mind that you get with insurance against the cost of a policy.

However, insurance for many entrepreneurs does tend to be an afterthought. They only think about insurance after something costly happens—they get sued by a customer, have to get their business equipment fixed, or get in trouble for something they didn't even think of. My message here is simple: Think ahead. Don't wait until something happens to get insurance. At least price out coverage for a package policy and the coverage you know you need now. This is usually enough to get you started. If you really don't know where to start, you may want to consider talking to an insurance broker early in building your business.

Tips for Getting to Go

1. Think about your insurance needs early. Get some coverage in place before you start selling your product or service. Most businesses will need a package policy of some type.
2. If you decide to talk to an insurance broker, be open and honest about your business operations. An insurance broker's job is to reach out to different insurance companies, explain your business to them, and recommend coverages to you. If they don't completely understand your business, you may get worse rates. If an insurance company does not understand the risk they are facing, it may agree to write the policy only for a very high premium.
3. Don't just pay the premium each year! Shop around and look for better rates, but always make sure your coverage keeps up with your business. Companies change a lot in the early years. As your business grows, your needs change. However, look around and consider your options. Just because you have been with an insurance company for many years, it does not mean you are always getting the best rate.

CHAPTER 6

Worry About the Big Stuff: You Need a Contract

It had been over two hours. I had successfully reached the bottom of my coffee cup, reorganized my papers, and made numerous doodles of cartoon characters from my childhood on my legal pad. The voice on the other side told me why he felt we had defined the term "insurance quote" inappropriately in our contract. We had already agreed on pricing, jurisdiction, and even how we would integrate into the software platform. I sat back in my chair and looked at the ceiling, wondering if this was really what I had in mind when I took a CFO role: sitting on the phone endlessly word-smithing contracts.

I exhaled loudly and quickly glanced at the phone to make sure I wasn't heard. I don't know what it was—too much coffee, too many "whereas" clauses, or just the pure desire to be free of this call—but something inside compelled me to lunge forward and take the phone off mute.

"Do you want to make a deal or not?" I felt the hairs on my neck stand up. I had blurted the words out so fast.

"Excuse me?" The voice on the other end asked in a perplexed tone.

In for a dime, in for a dollar, I thought to myself. Here goes nothing.

"Do you want to make a deal or not? I want to make a deal. I think we have agreed on the major terms. I don't care about the rest of this. Is this stuff we are discussing going to make or break this deal? If not, let's sign it and move on."

I was surprised at my boldness. However, after a brief pause, the voice on the other side agreed, and we hung up in about five minutes. Both sides signed the contract the next day. Deal done.

While I would never hold my actions up as a good way to conduct business (my words could have really hurt us), it does illustrate a lesson I learned very early on as a young executive at a startup company. If you are going to be successful getting a small business off the ground, you need to learn what to spend time on and what not to. Contracts are a necessary part of every business. They are important. They lay out the expectations in the agreement for both sides.

However, obsessing over minor, unimportant things can actually hurt a deal (and more importantly, the relationship you are trying to build). Knowing what you care about and what you don't in a contract negotiation can save you a lot of time. It also helps if you are willing to give. In my case, I had what I needed from this business partner. If he wanted to change the wording of how a term was defined, I didn't care. As soon as I made that known, we got it done quickly, both sides feeling good.

What are the elements of a valid contract?

In general, there are five elements that must be present for a contract to be valid:

- **Offer:** There needs to be an official offer made by one person. An offer can normally be revoked at any time.
- **Acceptance:** The other party must accept the offer made. (If the offeror has revoked an offer, it can no longer be accepted.) Sometimes, a person will change an offer. For example, they might say something like, "I am okay with everything you have outlined, but I would like to change the payment terms as well as the quantity." In certain instances, this might be construed as a counteroffer. The other party would then be asked to accept the counteroffer.
- **Consideration:** Consideration needs to be made on both sides as well. Consideration can be money, but it does not have to be. In many instances, consideration is simply promising to do something (or not do something). This promise would often be adequate consideration.[22]
- **Capacity:** Both sides to a contract must have capacity to enter a contract. This basically means both sides need to understand what they are doing. For example, a minor is considered by the law not to know what he/she is doing. For this reason, a contract made with a minor may be voidable by the minor. This means that the minor can choose to void the contract or abide by it. Elderly individuals also may not have capacity if they do not understand a contract.
- **Legal Purpose:** A contract must also be legal to be enforceable. A contract to do something illegal is not enforceable under the law.

If any of these elements are missing, there is no valid contract. Often, small business owners who are just getting started attempt to create

22 There are certain instances where the law will supply missing contract terms. For example, contracts that fall under the Uniform Commercial Code.

a contract for themselves by copying a template online. While it is possible to write a contract for yourself, it would need to have all the required elements to be valid. For more important contracts (like your client/customer contract), it is usually best to have an attorney draft an agreement for you. They can ensure the required elements are present and that your contract will hold up if you dispute with another company. If possible, engaging with an attorney specializing in your industry is wise. They will know what the best practices are for your industry.

How do I ensure my contract gets signed?

This is a tough one for a new business owner. If your contract terms are too one-sided, then your partner may never sign the deal (or it may have to go through multiple rounds of legal review). I have always found that shorter (more concise) contracts using plain language tend to be easier on both sides. However, the problem with a shorter contract is that it may not have all the legal details to protect you adequately. If you are concerned about this, a memorandum of understanding (also called "heads of terms") may be helpful.

A memorandum of understanding outlines the main parts of the agreement and is a precursor to a full contract. Both sides sign off to indicate their intentions to enter a full contract. Since you are agreeing on the major terms now, the full version of the contract becomes less intimidating later. You have any necessary conversations about the agreement upfront.

For customer contracts, keep in mind that your first contract may need to be revised. In the startups I have been a part of, our first contract was never the one we ultimately used. You figure out what works and what doesn't. You also figure out what questions your business partners have. This can help you determine where language or terms need to be revised.

Take It or Leave It

Certain types of contracts are essentially "take it or leave it" (sometimes referred to as a contract of adhesion). The recipient of the contract really can't negotiate any part of it. They can only choose to sign or not sign the terms presented. Many insurance policies and software agreements are this way. However, unless the law requires you to have this type of contract or you are in an industry where this is the norm, I wouldn't recommend being that rigid. If you are hard to deal with in the contract process, you will likely be hard to deal with in day-to-day business. You want to send a message that you will be easy to work with. The relationship with a partner generally begins not after the contract is signed, but when you begin negotiations.

How do I effectively negotiate a contract?

Like so many other things in business and life, preparation aids success. When you negotiate with a business partner, it is important to predict what terms they may likely want. What do you offer in your agreement that will be the most attractive to them? Are there items they have seemed interested in during preliminary discussions? What problem are they trying to solve by contracting with you? Once you understand what they will want, you need to consider which of these items you can give. If you can't give on a particular item, is there something you could offer as an alternative?

Once you have a sense of what the client is looking for, think about what's most important to you. Are there any dealbreakers? Are there any items that, if they do not give them to you, you would no longer want to do business with them? Making a list of the top three or five items I most want out of the contract has always helped me focus on my priorities.

If you can give on some items, you can likely get more of what you need. It is often best not to steamroll a business partner. If you get everything you want and they get nothing, it may lead to resentment once you start working together. I have always found it helpful to contemplate what would happen if I walked away from the deal as well. Think to yourself: What happens if this deal is not made? Are there alternatives? If not, you may find that you need to give a lot more ground to get an agreement in place. If you can walk away without losing much, then you may have the leverage to pursue what you want more freely. I have often found that even the negotiations that seem the most important will not break the business. There are normally other options, alternatives, and good reasons to walk if you need to.

Are contract terms should I watch out for?

- **Definitions:** If a contract has a separate definitions section, it is a good idea to skim it to ensure there are no unexpected terms. Understanding what constitutes a "late payment" or "early termination" can help clarify expectations and result in fewer surprises down the road.

- **Performance & Timing:** It is especially important to pay attention to terms discussing when certain milestones need to be reached. When do you need to complete your performance obligations? When can you expect your business partner to complete their portion? Logistically, is this possible on your side? Does it meet your needs?
- **Jurisdiction & Venue:** This is a section that is often glossed over by company representatives. They reason that as long as the jurisdiction is somewhere in the United States, the laws will be substantially similar. There are differences in laws not just between countries but even between states. However, this is only part of the issue. It is also important to think through what would happen in the event that a contract is actually challenged. Let's say that you have a company located in California, but you agreed that any disputes would be argued in a court located in New York. First, you might need to find an attorney licensed to practice in New York. Second, you may have the cost of traveling to New York (possibly multiple times) as well. The point is to think about the logistics of what you would need to do if there were a dispute.
- **Payment Terms:** Payment terms can vary significantly in contracts. If the contract calls for me to make a payment, I am always wary of short payment timeframes. For example, if you travel a lot, it may not be realistic for you to always make payments in fifteen days or less. Automatic payments are also something to be mindful of. While auto drafts can make payments easier, they are also easy to forget. Also, what happens in the case of a dispute? Is it easy to turn off the auto draft? What does this entail?

- **Indemnity Clauses:** Indemnification is the concept where one or both parties agree to cover the other's costs or damages in case of a breach of contract. This can get tricky. When does the indemnity clause come into play? Is the indemnity mutual? Or is indemnity only asked for from one side?

As a general word of advice on reviewing contracts for your business, you should never be afraid to ask questions. Good business partners want to make a deal and will do what they can to achieve mutual understanding. If you ever sense that someone is trying to "slip one by you," it is probably best to take a pass. A bad partner in the contract process normally leads to a bad partner overall. As my grandmother would say, trust your gut!

Which contracts require an attorney?

As mentioned, you can generally make or enter into contracts yourself. However, unless you are an attorney, this may not be a good idea. Normally, the more important a contract is, the more you need the help of an attorney. Just like everyone else, attorneys need to be paid for their services; there is a cost involved, but you can save yourself several headaches down the road.

When evaluating whether you need an attorney, you should consider your familiarity with particular types of contracts. If something unfamiliar to you, it may be best to ask for legal help. You should also consider the cost if something goes wrong. Is the money you would spend on an attorney worth paying now to avoid potential losses later? Finally, you should consider your budget. What can you afford? This is always an important consideration in any aspect of starting up a business. If you can't afford legal help, look for situations where free help may be available. If that is not an option, you can either work through the contract yourself or simply not enter it.

Can I create my own contracts?

As a business owner, you are allowed to draft your own contracts. There is nothing inherently wrong with this. As long as the five elements of the contract are present, you can create a binding agreement. Again, though, unless you are an attorney, you risk missing key aspects of the contract and facing liability.

Before resigning to writing your own sales contract from scratch, looking on reputable websites for templates and resources may be worthwhile. For example, some professional organizations have contract templates that their members can use. In the accounting and financial services industries, professional liability insurance companies often offer engagement letter templates that can be used. There are also online services that can draft contracts. The point here is to weigh the options. There may be more options available than initially appear.

Tips for Getting to Go

1. Whenever you look at a contract, pay attention to odd terms or anything out of the ordinary. Sometimes, it is just a drafting mistake, while other times, it is something worth your attention. Ask questions and think critically about what you are reading.
2. Never review a contract when you are tired! As a small business owner who reviews many agreements myself, I find it is never smart to review key documents when your eyes are likely

to skip over relevant details. No contract is so critical that you can't wait to sign it until the next morning!

3. Never be afraid to walk away. Especially early on in a business's existence, it may be difficult to say no to deals. You are often trying to gain traction in any way you can. It is normal to feel like an opportunity now will never come your way again. However, that's usually not the case. Opportunities come again if you are patient. Don't aim for the perfect deal (it probably doesn't exist); obsessing over insignificant elements can impair your business's ability to move forward. However, refusing to enter into a deal for the right reasons can open you up to better opportunities in the long run!

CHAPTER 7

This Stinks: You Need to Pay Taxes

Note: While every effort has been made at the time of this writing to give accurate and helpful information, it should be noted that tax laws change all the time. Therefore, this chapter is only meant to provide an overview of the issues at hand. It is always best to consult with a tax accountant or tax attorney if you have questions on current laws, recent changes, or your specific circumstances.

I have always volunteered in my community. It helps me keep perspective on what is most meaningful in life. Whether it has been coaching junior soccer, building houses for those who can't afford it, or counseling teachers on their retirement plans, there is something deeply satisfying about helping someone for its own sake.

While there are many charities I enjoy volunteering for, Junior Achievement has to be my favorite. Having open and honest dialogue with younger people about budgeting, the importance of saving, and what insurance is appeals to the financial advisor in me.

"This stinks!" A young voice from the back of the room exclaimed. He just had a few more of his goldfish crackers taken away. He was learning how taxes worked.

"Yes, but everyone has to pay taxes," I said in my best elementary-school-teacher voice.

"But why do *I* have to pay taxes?"

"Well, because taxes are how we pay for schools, roads, and the big sports stadiums. If the government doesn't take taxes, it can't pay for those things." I could tell he wasn't convinced.

After thinking for a minute, he said firmly, "I will just stay home!"

My young pupil's words echo how many entrepreneurs feel when they first learn about all the taxes they need to pay from the second they open. They feel so overwhelmed and taken advantage of by the system in place that they wish they could just stay home!

The reality, though, is that we all must pay taxes. I will not try to convince you that the system is fair or great in all cases. However, if you know what to expect, it can be easier to navigate. You don't need to be a tax expert to know what you need to file. You just need to understand some of the common taxes out there and when they might be an issue.

Is nexus a brand of chocolate?

No. Nestle is a food and beverage company that makes cocoa. Nexus is a legal term that describes the connection a jurisdiction (country, state, or city) needs to have with your business before taxing it. Our tax system is built on the idea that a jurisdiction needs to have a logical connection with a company before assessing a tax. Nexus appeals to our sense of fairness. Think about it. If this were not the case, my business could be taxed by a state in which I had never set foot or sold a product. This system is fair in that we are only taxed where we do business.

How much activity it takes for us to be held liable for a tax depends on the jurisdiction and the type of tax. In other words, nexus is not just one thing. It can vary from tax to tax or jurisdiction to jurisdiction. What makes a company liable for sales tax in one state may not be the same set of criteria that make it liable for income taxes in the same state. What makes a company liable for sales tax in one state may not make it liable for sales tax in another state. In the following pages, we will discuss what makes you liable for a particular tax. However, different jurisdictions have different rules. If you are uncomfortable navigating the rules, always check with a tax professional. After reading this chapter, you will be able to ask better questions and get better answers.

What are sales and use taxes?

Sales and use taxes are similar conceptually, but they are actually two different things. Sales tax is generally assessed when a customer buys goods or products from you. You report to the state how much you have sold your products for during the tax period on a sales tax return. (Some states allow the returns to be done electronically on their website.) A formula will then be used (normally a percentage) to figure out how much you will need to give the state for sales tax. In most cases, sales tax returns are due monthly, and a late fee may be assessed if you file or pay late. Sales taxes are assessed against the company that sells the product.

While sales taxes are typically assessed on sales of tangible products (things you can touch), a use tax is assessed against the consumer for services or products in a given state. Use taxes will typically only apply when a sales tax has not been paid for that product already. For example, let's say that your business is located in State A and that State A does *not* have a sales tax. You sell a product to a customer who lives in State B. State B *does* have a sales tax. However, the customer bought the product from you in State A, so they have not paid any sales tax. The customer intends to use the product in State B, where they live. In this instance, a use tax would need to be paid in State B.

What makes this matter more confusing is that some jurisdictions use the term sales and use tax interchangeably. Also, while it is generally true that sales and use taxes only apply to tangible goods, some states apply these taxes to intangible products, Internet-based products, and even some services. It is enough to make a new business owner's head spin!

My advice to new business owners in this area is always the same: Look at the state's laws or sales tax return instructions. See if your product or service is something that a tax is assessed against. If it is, you will normally need to register with the State Department of Taxation and obtain a sales and use tax account. Sales and use taxes are normally due each month, so you will want to get a handle on this quickly.

What if I only make a few sales in the state?

In most states, there is a minimum threshold that you must exceed before you need to start filing and paying sales and use tax (that is, before you have nexus). For example, you may not need to file a sales and use tax return until you reach two hundred individual sales and at least $100,000 in revenue in a state.[23]

To determine which state laws to consult: for services, you generally look at where the services are performed; for products, you normally look at where the customer is located.[24] For example, let's say your business is located in State A. You perform a service for a customer in State B and charge them $1,000. This would count as one transaction for $1,000 for State B. If State B says that your service is subject to sales and use tax, you would begin filing returns and paying taxes in State B once you meet State B's minimum threshold. As another example, let's say you sell a product to someone in State C for $1,000. This would likewise be considered one transaction for $1,000 sourced to State C.

It is important to remember that different states have different thresholds. If you plan to sell in multiple states, you must follow the rules for each state. Also, it should be clear that good recordkeeping is the key to complying with the regulations. If you don't know where your customers are located, you won't be able to meet the requirements easily. Therefore, it is best to set up good systems from the start.

What if I sell on a website like Amazon or Etsy?

This is another place where states are different. In some states, the marketplace facilitator (Amazon or Etsy) is expected to file the sales tax return. They would collect the tax from customers who buy your

---

23 This is one of the most common thresholds after the Wayfair decision in 2018. However, not every state follows this threshold.

24 This is a general rule. Again, *every* state is different. You need to either read the state laws for yourself or hire a good CPA who is well-versed in the tax laws of the states in which you operate.

products and then remit the sales tax to the state. In other states, the small business (you) would be expected to file and remit any sales taxes. This is a tricky area within state tax laws. If you decide to do this, talk to a tax accountant who specializes in these areas and build the cost of compliance into the pricing of your product or service.

Can a CPA handle this for me?

This is probably the most common question I get from new business owners once they start to see the murkiness of many state sales tax laws. While there is nothing wrong with having a CPA take care of your sales tax reporting and filings, you will still need to supply the CPA with all of the information for the returns.

As a CPA who has been in practice for many years, I know this is a common problem when an engagement starts: the client assumes their CPA will handle everything, so they neglect essential tracking or record-keeping. However, unless your CPA is in the office with you every day, it is important to remember that they have no way of tracking your sales, where your customers are, or how much you are selling. You will still need to record this information so that you can have it ready once your CPA asks for it. I advise working with the CPA to develop a process that will be as easy as possible for both of you. They can help you establish the best way to capture the information upfront.

What if I have employees?

We have discussed how self-employment taxes work in an earlier chapter. However, if you have employees, you will need to file and pay payroll taxes for them. You will also need to follow the withholding rules for each state. If you look at a paystub, you will generally see four different taxes an employer pays: Social Security, Medicare, federal income tax withholding, and state income tax withholding. You may have also heard about unemployment taxes. Let's talk about each of these.

Payroll Taxes: Social Security & Medicare

For federal tax purposes, there are two types of payroll taxes: Social Security and Medicare. Each employee pays a 6.2% Social Security tax and a 1.45% Medicare tax on their wages. Each employer pays a matching amount of tax on the same wages. For example, let's say you pay your employee $1,000 in wages. Your employee would pay $62 in Social Security taxes ($1,000 x 6.2% = $62) and $14.50 in Medicare taxes ($1,000 x 1.45% = $14.50). These amounts would be withheld from their paycheck. The employer would owe a matching amount of each tax: $62 for Social Security taxes and $14.50 for Medicare taxes on the same $1,000 in wages that you paid your employee.[25]

Unemployment Taxes: Federal & State Unemployment

You will also likely need to pay unemployment taxes on your employees' wages as well. Unlike Social Security and Medicare, only the employer pays unemployment taxes, not the employee. Unemployment is a federal program administered by each state. As a result, you will normally pay a portion of unemployment taxes to the federal government and a portion to the state government. Unemployment is

25 Even though the employee pays for their share of Social Security and Medicare taxes, the employer remits these taxes to the federal government (along with the employer side of these taxes and any federal withholding) – not the employee.

often paid to the employee's state of residence, but not always. State laws differ in this area.

You report your calculation of federal unemployment taxes on Form 940. Form 940 is normally due by January 31st each year. States will have their own forms for reporting unemployment taxes.

Withholding: Federal Income Taxes & State Income Taxes

For each employee, you will also need to withhold state income taxes on their behalf. When an employee starts working for you, you should ask them to fill out a Form W-4. Form W-4 will show the employee's filing status (Married Filing Jointly, Single, etc.). This tells you (the employer) how much you should withhold for federal taxes for that employee. The IRS publishes tables in Publication 15-T telling the correct amount of federal income tax withholding that should be taken from each employee's check. An example from one of the tables is shown in the following figure. You will also see that there are different tables to reference depending on the frequency with which you run payroll. The table below assumes that payroll is run on a weekly basis.

It is important to remember that the withholding amounts in the table are adjusted by the IRS each year for inflation (the table above is from 2024). You should also know that if a tax law changes the tax rates, the IRS may need to change the tables as well.

States with an income tax for individuals will normally follow a similar process. States often have their own version of the Form W-4 to indicate how much should be withheld from the employee's wages for state income taxes. Tables are generally published each year for

WEEKLY Payroll Period							
If the Adjusted Wage Amount (line 1h) is		Married Filing Jointly		Head of Household		Single or Married Filing Separately	
At least	But less than	Standard withholding	Form W-4, Step 2, Checkbox withholding	Standard withholding	Form W-4, Step 2, Checkbox withholding	Standard withholding	Form W-4, Step 2, Checkbox withholding
		The Tentative Withholding Amount is:					
$0	$145	$0	$0	$0	$0	$0	$0
$145	$155	$0	$0	$0	$0	$0	$1
$155	$165	$0	$0	$0	$0	$0	$2
$165	$175	$0	$0	$0	$0	$0	$3
$175	$185	$0	$0	$0	$0	$0	$4
$185	$195	$0	$0	$0	$0	$0	$5
$195	$205	$0	$0	$0	$0	$0	$6
$205	$215	$0	$0	$0	$0	$0	$7
$215	$225	$0	$0	$0	$1	$0	$8
$225	$235	$0	$0	$0	$2	$0	$9
$235	$245	$0	$0	$0	$3	$0	$10
$245	$255	$0	$0	$0	$4	$0	$11
$255	$265	$0	$0	$0	$5	$0	$12
$265	$275	$0	$0	$0	$6	$0	$13
$275	$285	$0	$0	$0	$7	$0	$15
$285	$295	$0	$1	$0	$8	$1	$16
$295	$305	$0	$2	$0	$9	$2	$17
$305	$315	$0	$3	$0	$10	$3	$18
$315	$325	$0	$4	$0	$11	$4	$19
$325	$335	$0	$5	$0	$12	$5	$21
$335	$345	$0	$6	$0	$13	$6	$22
$345	$355	$0	$7	$0	$14	$7	$23
$355	$365	$0	$8	$0	$15	$8	$24

each state, just like at the federal level. You typically need to withhold state taxes in any state where an employee works.[26]

26 State income tax withholding is a highly complex area of the tax law. Some states like New York follow very different rules from the ones we mentioned above. It is even possible to withhold taxes in more than one state for the same employee.

How do tax payments get to the government?

At this point, you may be wondering how the tax money gets to the federal government. The short answer is that you calculate how much you owe and send it to them electronically.

You use Form 941 to calculate how much you need to send the federal government. You will need to send them the total of the five taxes added together:

- Social Security Tax (employee portion)
- Social Security Tax (employer portion)
- Medicare Tax (employee portion)
- Medicare Tax (employer portion)
- Federal Income Tax Withheld (from the employee's paycheck)

Imagine you pay your employee $1,000 in wages. As we calculated above, the employee would have $62 withheld for their share of Social Security taxes and $14.50 withheld for their share of Medicare taxes. Let's also assume that we have read this employee's W-4 and, according to the IRS tables, we need to withhold $200 for federal income taxes from this employee's check. For simplicity, we will assume that this employee lives and works in a state with no state income tax. Therefore, we would pay the employee $723.50 ($1000 - $62 - $14.50 - $200 = $723.50).[27] This would be their paycheck. We collect the withholdings from the employee and report them on the Form 941 (along with the employer's share of Social Security and Medicare). In

27 This assumes the employee is not paying for any benefits, which is exceedingly rare since employees at many companies pay for their own health insurance and life insurance and make contributions to their 401(k). However, we are trying to keep this example simple to illustrate how payroll taxes work. Just remember that in real life, it is a little bit more complicated than our example here.

our example, the calculation would look something like this:

Social Security Tax (employee portion) = $62.00

Social Security Tax (employer portion) = $62.00

Medicare Tax (employee portion) = $14.50

Medicare Tax (employer portion) = $14.50

Federal Income Tax Withheld (from the employee's paycheck) = $200

Total amount to be sent to the federal government = $353.00

You would then send the federal government a payment using the Electronic Federal Tax Payment System (EFTPS) for $353.00. To use EFTPS, you must first apply to the IRS and set up an account. Therefore, it is useful to get EFTPS set up well before you need to run your first payroll.

I should mention a few logistics here before we keep going. First, the example above assumes we only have one employee on payroll. If we had many employees, we would need to total all the wages we paid, calculate the combined withholding amount, and report it on Form 941. Also, Form 941 generally covers an entire quarter of payroll. Our example above assumes that we only had one payroll during the quarter. In real life, you would probably have many payrolls that you ran during the quarter. Form 941 would report all the wages and withholdings calculated for the quarter. This form is only for federal withholdings, too. States often have a similar system for paying state withholdings.

Finally, it should be noted that the frequency of your payroll deposits depends on your payroll size (in terms of dollars). In certain instances, you may need to make a payroll deposit the next day after running payroll. It is important to stay on top of these deadlines since not making deposits can result in severe IRS penalties—for you personally (if you are running your own payroll) and for the company.

Can a CPA or payroll service run payroll for me?

Absolutely. In fact, due to the myriad logistical issues (and potential IRS penalties), many companies outsource payroll. Before doing this, though, you should consider a few things. First, it is important to remember that you are always held responsible for your payroll, even if you outsource it to another firm. For example, let's say your payroll provider does not file Form 941 on time. You would still be responsible for paying the late filing penalty. This is very similar to if an employee of yours messes up a job for a customer. You are ultimately still responsible since you are the employer.

Second, there are different levels of service when it comes to payroll providers. Some payroll providers only offer a web-based platform. Essentially, you do everything: You enter the payroll information for each check. Payroll tax filings may be done automatically, but you are responsible for any issues that arise. Your fee is often very low, since you only pay for the right to use their software. On the other hand, you may have a payroll provider that offers more full-scale service. They run payroll for you, make sure tax filings are made, and serve as a resource for questions. They may also make suggestions on ways to make tax compliance easier. There are many other options on the spectrum between these two models.[28]

For these reasons, the decision to engage a payroll provider should never be taken lightly. Don't pay attention to just fees. While fees are important, you need a payroll provider you can trust to make the filings and do the work that you need. You should also obtain

28 It is important to note that not every CPA firm offers payroll services. CPA firms tend to specialize in certain areas, such as tax, audit, or payroll. My own CPA firm has never offered payroll to clients!

a clear understanding of what the payroll company will be offering and what you are expected to do. Again, not all payroll providers offer the same level of service. If you are okay doing the bulk of the payroll entry yourself, perhaps you only need a web-based platform. If you prefer to stay out of payroll as much as possible, you will need a higher service level.

Finally, I urge you to think through what would happen if you had a problem. For example, would the firm that you hired be able to help you with an IRS notice? What happens if the platform is not working properly? While there is no "correct" answer to any of these questions, it is important to examine them and figure out how you feel about them before signing an engagement letter.

What is a wage report?

Just like at the federal level, there are certain payroll tax filings that need to be made at the state level. We already mentioned the need to file a state unemployment report (see above). Another common report is a state wage report. In many states, a company will need to report how much it paid to employees in that state. The state will then assess a tax based on a percentage of wages. In many cases, wage reports must be filed quarterly (like the Form 941 at the federal level) online or via paper filing.

What about real estate & personal property taxes?

Just like individuals, real estate taxes are paid by businesses based on the location of their offices, factories, or other buildings. If you have a separate place of business, you will likely need to pay real estate taxes on this location. If you rent your office, it is possible that the owner of the building may pay the real estate taxes on your location for you.

Personal property taxes are typically assessed by a city or county. In many cases, the tax charged to the business is based on the value of the business property located there. For example, Greenfield County might charge a personal property tax based on the value of any business property located in Greenfield County but not on any business property located in a neighboring county.

How could I forget about income taxes?

Just like individuals, businesses may also need to pay income taxes. As mentioned in the chapter on entity types, there are two basic types of tax structures for federal tax purposes: pass-throughs and stand-alones. A pass-through entity generally does not pay any taxes. It simply passes the items of income, deduction, gains, losses, and credits through to the individual owners. The individual owners then add those items to their tax items on their personal income tax returns. They pay taxes at their individual rate. There are many types of pass-through entities. As discussed in the chapter on entity types, many of them require their own tax return. However, a sole proprietorship does not. There is only one type of stand-alone entity for federal tax purposes, and that is the C corporation. A C corporation files its own tax return and pays its taxes at its tax rate.

Many states also have an income tax return that needs to be filed for a business. Oftentimes, state laws are close to the federal laws for businesses in terms of when a company needs to file. A word of caution should be said here, though. Some states might require disregarded entities, like single-member LLCs, to file their own tax return at the state level (even though this would generally not be required for federal tax purposes).

The good news is that regardless of your business's entity type, a few commonalities apply to most situations. Most small businesses are on a cash basis. This means they will declare income on the tax return in the same year that a customer pays them. It also means that you can take deductions in the year that you pay for items as well.[29] This means that one way to reduce your tax bill is to pay for some things before the tax year ends. You pay taxes on net income from your business. If you have more expenses (deductions), you will reduce your net income.

What can I deduct?

Regardless of entity type, the IRS generally allows you to deduct any business expense that is ordinary, necessary, and reasonable in the circumstances. While there are some expenses with additional requirements (more on that later), most things we spend money on for our business are deductible. The one requirement is to keep expenses reasonable for the business you are in. For example, a hammer and screwdriver are probably deductible for a contractor, but not if you are an attorney. Similarly, cattle feed is deductible for a dairy farmer, but that same expenditure would likely not be available as a write-off to a plumber. All business expenses need to be reasonable in the circumstances for the given business.

There are a few expenses that go against this principle. For example, in nearly all instances, political contributions are not deductible. The same applies to fines and penalties assessed by the IRS against

29 There are some limitations on this. For example, if you prepay for something too far in advance (where the benefit typically extends beyond 12 months), it is not deductible at the time you pay for it.

you, since such things would never be considered "ordinary or necessary" for any business. However, almost every other normal business expense is deductible.

One element the IRS normally wants to see is substantiation. In other words, for every deduction you take, you need to be able to show that you actually spent the money on something business-related. This usually means keeping receipts, cancelled checks, or credit card transaction records. You should also try to classify the expenses into the type of business expense they are—office supplies, inventory, legal fees, etc. Doing this will help you recognize the business purpose of the expenditure. It will also prove useful if you ever get audited.

Strict substantiation? That sounds scary.

I have always been a rule follower. When I was a kid, I distinctly remember coloring between the lines and always sitting at the desk I was supposed to. When learning how to bake cupcakes for the first time, I remember meticulously following the recipe, convinced that if I messed up, the world would end and every cupcake connoisseur would scorn me. However, my classmates were less encumbered by strict measurements. My young grade school mind was appalled when a friend simply threw some additional sugar into the batter without measuring. He looked at me and shrugged. "Good enough," he said and moved on.

As I have gotten older, I have realized that not everything requires perfection. You can put a bit more sugar into your cake batter, and the recipe will come out fine (even better, sometimes). You can get away with some uneven strokes when painting your bedroom.

You can even arrive at a meeting a few minutes late, and no one really notices. However, this is not true for everything in this world. On the tax return, the IRS expects certain rules to be followed and items to be accurate to the dollar.

I am going to let you in on a secret. Are you ready for it? The IRS knows about all the business deductions people tend to "fudge" on. They know that people occasionally exaggerate their business miles. They also know try to deduct meals that aren't related to business. They are even aware that some nefarious individuals might say something is a business travel expense when it was actually for a personal vacation!

In all seriousness, there are certain types of deductions that are easy to manipulate. As a result, these deductions are subject to "strict substantiation" rules. In other words, you can't deduct these things on your tax return unless you follow the documentation requirements to the letter. Probably the three most common deductions subject to strict substantiation requirements are business miles, business meals, and travel costs.[30] Let's look briefly at each of them:

Business Miles

In Tax Land, there are three different types of mileage: personal miles, commuting miles, and business miles. Out of the three, only business miles are deductible. While personal miles are generally any miles that don't fit in the other two categories, discerning between business miles and commuting miles is a bit more difficult. The miles from home to work, as well as the drive from work to home, are commuting miles. Once I am at the office, mileage to go see clients, run ordinary

30 Technically, strict substantiation requirements are discussed in Sec 274(d) and don't include business miles per se. However, in most cases, deductions related to business miles must be substantiated in a similar way to the other items discussed in Sec 274(d). If you don't have the right elements in the business mileage log, the IRS will normally just deny the deduction.

and necessary business errands, or attend educational events is all considered to be business miles. Taxpayers can usually deduct their business miles multiplied by a standard rate.[31] Alternatively, they can deduct the actual expenses they incur using their vehicle.[32]

While this sounds simple, there are several caveats to remember. First, even though the only deductible miles are business miles, the taxpayer must keep track of all three types. This can be done using an app or just a notebook and a pen. Regardless of the recordkeeping method you choose, you need to declare how many miles you had in each category on the tax return (business, commuting, and personal).[33] For business miles, you should put together a log. The log should include the date, business miles traveled, and the purpose of the trip (attend client meeting, meet with business partner, etc.). Tracking commuting miles does not need to be done in a log, but one should generally know how long the trip is from home to work and work to home each day. Most people work about two hundred and fifty days each year.[34] Take your average daily round trip to work each day and multiply it by two hundred and fifty; this should be about what your commuting miles are for the year. Finally, personal miles may be tracked by simply looking at the odometer in your car at the beginning and end of the year. If you subtract your beginning odometer reading from your ending odometer reading, this will give you the total miles you drove during the year. You then subtract commuting

---

31 The standard mileage rate normally changes each year due to inflation. In 2025, it is seventy cents per mile.

32 Keep in mind that only the business portion of the vehicle expenses is deductible. So, if you use your vehicle 50% of the time for business and 50% for personal use, then only half of your actual expenses would be deductible.

33 Technically, the tax return asks for "Other" miles. However, this would be the same thing as personal miles, since personal miles are not business miles or commuting miles.

34 This assumes someone works five days per week and fifty weeks out of the year. It assumes that they take two weeks off for vacation.

and business miles from this total to get your personal miles.

For example, let's say that you subtract your beginning odometer reading from your ending odometer reading, and you see that you drove 12,000 miles during the year. You kept a mileage log, so you know that you had 3,000 business miles during the year. You also know that you had 1,000 commuting miles. Therefore, your personal miles would be 8,000 (12,000 – 3,000 – 1,000 = 8,000).

While it's tempting to do so, the log should not be estimated or "reconstructed" after the fact. The IRS wants you to keep the log throughout the year. Since business miles are subject to strict substantiation requirements, if a log cannot be produced to document the business mileage, the IRS may not allow the deduction.

Many taxpayers found this out during the pandemic. Even though many cities were shut down nationwide, bold taxpayers seeking to lower their taxable income took large mileage deductions (often in round numbers, like 2,000 business miles). The IRS was quick to send out letters asking for a business mileage log to support the deductions. The moral of the story: Don't guess; keep documentation!

Third, it is difficult (but not impossible) to have all business miles. In today's modern world, many people work from home. If you work from home and only use the car for business-related purposes, then you would have no commuting or personal miles. All miles would be business miles in this rare case. However, this is only possible if the person has a vehicle that is only used for business.

Fourth, be aware that certain professions have special rules regarding mileage. For example, if you are constantly traveling to different job sites or are a long-haul trucker, the rules are a bit different. For most everyone else, though, the rules above will apply.

Business Meals

Business meals are another area that the IRS deems ripe for abuse. Therefore, only 50% of the cost of the business meal is deductible. Also, documentation of who you are meeting and the business purpose of the meeting is important. You'll also want to keep your receipt showing the amount, time, and date. Each of these elements is necessary to meet the strict substantiation requirements. If you ever receive an IRS letter, this is what you would be asked to produce to justify your deduction for business meals.

It is important to remember that all business deductions must be reasonable in the circumstances. In other words, overly lavish meals should be avoided. This doesn't mean that you can't take a client out for a steak dinner, but it does mean that too many extravagant meals may result in a deduction being denied. Also, while sending someone a meal using a delivery service (Uber Eats, Door Dash, Grub Hub, etc.) became popular during the pandemic and can be a great gesture, you need to be present at the business meal for it to be deductible.[35] Remember, the reason why a business meal is deductible is that there is a business element being discussed over the meal.

Finally, while food and entertainment often go together when trying to impress clients, entertainment expenses are no longer deductible. This change was made several years ago. Now, if I decide to take a client out to a baseball game and pay for a hot dog lunch, only half the cost of the hot dog lunch would be deductible. The cost of the ticket would not be deductible, nor the parking, nor any other entertainment costs. Always get a separate receipt for the meals portion, so you can at least get a 50% deduction for that part.[36]

---

35 This could potentially be a business gift, but the IRS places several limits around what may be deducted as a business gift as well.

36 In the case of an all-inclusive cost, everything would be considered nondeductible. It is only when the cost of meals can be separated and isolated from the entertainment costs that the meals are 50% deductible.

Travel Costs

Even in a world where video conferencing is now the norm, it is not unusual for someone to travel for business purposes. This is another area where the strict substantiation requirements apply. You need to ensure that you document the amount, time, place, and business purpose of each expense.[37] This might mean obtaining receipts from ridesharing services, hotel invoices, receipts from meals, and e-bills for airline tickets. Again, the point here (as with all items subject to strict substantiation) is that you want to make sure you can prove the cost is a legitimate business expense. For this reason, you also want to make sure the main purpose of the trip is business (not a personal vacation). If there are too many elements of personal pleasure, the deduction may be denied.

Where do I need to file?

Any business located in the United States—or selling products or services to people in the United States—has to file a federal tax return. That's the easy part. Figuring out which states your business needs to file in is more difficult. This gets back to the idea of nexus we talked about earlier. If a business has nexus with a state, it needs to file a tax return there.

Similarly to what we saw for sales tax purposes, companies normally need to file a return in the states where they have their product or service. Each state has its own way of calculating how much income needs to be sourced to a particular state. In general, income is apportioned for state tax purposes. Where this becomes particularly complex is that it is possible (and very common) for multiple states

37 Reg 1.274-5A(b)(2)

to tax the same dollar of sales from a company. This is because the formulas that each state uses are non-uniform. As a result, income is not apportioned consistently from one state to the next, and as a result, it could get taxed more than once.

Luckily, when the same dollar of income is taxed twice, most states offer an offsetting credit. A credit is a dollar-for-dollar reduction in a company's tax liability. For example, let's say that a company has $100 in sales. The sales are taxed in the company's home state, State A, at a rate of 25%. The same $100 in sales is taxed at 15% in State B, a neighboring state where the company has several customers. The company would pay $15 in state income taxes in State B ($100 x 15% = $15). It would also pay $25 in state income taxes in State A ($100 x 25% = $25). However, with the offsetting credit, the company would be able to reduce its $25 tax bill in its home state by $15 (the amount of taxes it paid to another state). Therefore, it would only owe $10 in State A, rather than the full $25. The credit for taxes paid to another state is a way of mitigating the damaging effects of the same dollar being taxed multiple times. While the calculation can be more complex than what we have demonstrated here, in all cases, the credit is welcome relief for companies that operate in more than one state.

What will my income tax preparer need from me?

As my young friend from the beginning of the chapter rightly said, taxes do stink! We have shown in this chapter some of the complexities you may encounter by trying to tackle parts of your tax filings on your own. For this reason, most entrepreneurs choose to have someone else prepare their income tax returns for them. If nothing else, this allows you to bounce ideas off another person and affords you more time to pursue additional clients and market your product. However, like what we have seen with other parts of tax compliance, outsourcing your income taxes to a tax preparer does not relieve you of everything.

First, you need to supply your tax preparer with a balance sheet and income statement each year. A balance sheet shows the following as of the last day of the tax year:

- **Assets:** items that the company owns
- **Liabilities:** debts that the company owes
- **Equity or Capital:** the owner's share of the assets after all liabilities are paid (normally calculated as assets minus liabilities)

You will also need to supply them with an income statement, which shows the following for the last year:

- **Revenues or Income:** the amounts the company has earned from selling its product or service
- **Expenses:** expenditures that the company has incurred by conducting business

The balance sheet and income statement are the primary sources of information for what gets entered on the company's tax return. It also alerts your tax preparer to what has happened with the company during the year.

It is possible to have your tax preparer do your bookkeeping throughout the year. To do this, they would need copies of your business bank statements, credit card statements, and possibly copies of cancelled checks. This can help streamline the tax preparation process because your preparer can ask questions about transactions on an ongoing basis throughout the year (rather than asking everything once tax season starts). However, like anything else in business, outsourcing your bookkeeping is an additional cost. There are many apps and software programs that can make it easier to do your accounting yourself, but you have to stay on top of it and feel comfortable with it. If you don't feel comfortable doing your own bookkeeping, I would strongly consider outsourcing it.

Second, in addition to providing a balance sheet and income statement, your tax preparer will probably ask you to provide substantiation for certain transactions (see the section on strict substantiation above) and fill out a questionnaire. The questionnaire will ask you about significant changes from one year to the next. It will also ask you to confirm basic information about your business, such as its legal name and tax ID.

Third, you will be asked to sign an engagement letter. Engagement letters are common throughout the accounting industry. While they can be overwhelming with multiple pages, they are helpful in presenting what your tax preparer will do and what you need to do. Aside from fee structure, look at what happens if you get an IRS letter. Is this something you are responsible for taking care of? Or is this part of your tax preparation fee? Tax practitioners have different policies and procedures. Remember that the IRS can ultimately send an audit letter to whoever it chooses. No tax preparer can ever guarantee that you will never get audited or receive a letter from a taxing authority. This makes it even more important to make sure you know what to expect if that time comes for you.

Fourth, if you want to keep your income tax preparation fees to a minimum, you should have your receipts and accounting records in order before you hand them over to your preparer. You should also have any questionnaires filled out as much as possible. This will save your preparer time, which means you will probably save some money.

Tips for Getting to Go

1. Tax compliance is something every business owner must deal with. Get on top of it quickly. You can avoid a lot of headaches by doing your homework ahead of time and getting a general idea of what you need to file with which regulatory authorities.
2. If you decide to outsource some (or all) of your accounting and tax compliance, it is normally best to develop a relationship with a professional early. The more they know about your business, the more they can help you when you need it.
3. When picking a tax preparer, it is important to choose someone with whom you feel comfortable talking. If you don't feel like you can ask them a question, they are probably not a good match for you.

CHAPTER 8

You Can't Be Everywhere: You Need to Hire

Note: While every effort has been made at the time of this writing to give accurate and helpful information, it should be noted that tax laws change all of the time. Therefore, this chapter is only meant to give you an overview of the issues at hand. It is always best to consult with a tax accountant or tax attorney if you have questions on current law, recent changes, or your specific circumstances.

"People." That was my answer to a journalist who was interviewing me for a story she was doing on the challenges of building a small business from scratch. I don't think she was expecting a one-word answer when she asked me to describe the hardest thing to get right. However, in all honesty, I don't think I could have said anything more accurate or appropriate.

"Can you elaborate?" she asked me in an expectant tone.

"People are difficult to predict. You may be able to predict how customers will react to a product. You may be able to figure out where your lowest-cost options are for operations. However, it is hard to truly understand anyone in a one-hour interview. You could interview them ten times and still be surprised by something they do. It is also really hard to predict who will get along with who, and how all the pieces will fit into the mold of what you are trying to build. The toughest thing about building a business is the people."

That part of the interview never got published. The interviewer was more interested in my views on the world economy and philosophy on management. However, I still remember clearly what I said. In my opinion, she missed the story. Even in today's age of automation and speed, the fact is that all businesses win and lose based on the people they have—and whether that team can come together and conquer mountains.

In my experience dealing with entrepreneurs, people are often the furthest thing from their minds initially. They are concerned with saving money, getting the word out about their product, and looking at how they can control their own destiny. As someone who admittedly loves to work and see business success, I understand this feeling better than most. However, the problem is that there is only so much *you.* At some point, you must either be content with what you can do as an individual or hire someone to help. While neither choice is bad, the problem with not hiring is that it limits the capacity and growth possibilities for your business. For this reason, most business owners choose to hire some help.

When is the right time to hire?

This is the main question every new business owner struggles with. There are several issues that compound this problem:

Hiring takes time.

I am not sure I have ever hired at exactly the right time. If you hire too early, you may not have enough work for the person to do (and you may waste some money). If you hire too late, then you risk burning yourself (or others on your staff) out. It is also tough to predict how long the hiring process will take. Some positions can be filled in a matter of days, while others can take months to fill.

You can usually outsource the skills you don't have.

In most cases, you can outsource the skills you don't have. If you are not a marketing person, you can hire a marketing firm. If you are not an accounting person, you can hire a CPA firm. If you are not an IT person, you can outsource your technology needs. In fact, it may be possible to build a firm where you are the only employee and all the company's functions are outsourced! However, the problem with outsourcing is that it gets expensive. If you are using an outside resource too much, it may become cheaper to hire someone (even with all the payroll and benefits costs). Not to mention that when you utilize outside resources, you are one client of many to that group. While this may be okay for some functions, it may not be okay for others. For certain functions, you may need to be a higher priority.

You may be able to hire part-time.

Hiring part-time can be a good alternative when money is tight and the need is not quite enough to warrant a full-time position. In certain instances, hiring part-time can work well for both the worker and the employer. An employee who needs more time in his/her schedule for family, school, or other activities may be the perfect fit.

However, like outsourcing, there are downsides to hiring part-time. The person may not be able to (or not want to) make your business a high enough priority. This may be okay, or it may hinder growth. I have found that this varies from one situation to the next and depends on the worker. Before hiring someone part-time, you should also consider when you need the person. Are there particular times when you know you will need their help? If so, you will need to ensure they can meet your scheduling needs.

All of this is to say that trying to hire at precisely the right time is very difficult. What I have found to be the most helpful is to consider your vision for the company, and think about whether the person fits in. In other words, ask yourself: Why did you go out on your own? What was your vision for this company? If you were doing it simply to provide for yourself and create work only for you, it may not be a good idea to hire. However, if you envision a company that has employees and is looking to grow, where does this person fit in? Do they fit into your long-term plans? If you can see them within your long-term vision for your own firm, then it is probably time to hire.

Employee vs. independent contractor—what's the difference?

From an IRS and Department of Labor (DOL) perspective, this is a critical question. An employee is involved in the day-to-day operations of your business. They participate in meetings, are obligated to do certain training, and are subject to your company's rules. They often have an exclusive (or semi-exclusive) working relationship with your firm. An independent contractor is someone who works with other firms or clients and ultimately uses much of their own equipment and staff to perform tasks. A vendor may be an independent contractor.

While the terms sound similar, the differences between the two from an IRS and DOL perspective are significant. As discussed in the chapter on taxes, you withhold and pay payroll taxes on employee wages. Employees are also entitled to company benefits and may participate in the company retirement plan. There are no requirements for independent contractors to do any of these things. There are no requirements to withhold taxes for independent contractors. Independent contractors cannot participate in the 401(k) or be entitled to company benefits.

For this reason, there is a significant incentive for employers to classify workers as independent contractors. Both the IRS and the DOL know this. As a result, there are certain factors both groups look at when determining whether a worker is an employee or independent contractor. The IRS uses a twenty-factor test to make this determination:[38]

1. **Instructions:** An employee receives instructions from an employer and must comply with them. An independent contractor generally has more freedom to determine how the work is done.
2. **Training:** Employees typically receive very specific training on the systems and processes used by employers. This is not as true with independent contractors.
3. **Integration:** Employees are more integrated into the day-to-day operations of the employer. They attend company-mandated meetings and are part of strategic and operational discussions. This is not the case with independent contractors. Independent contractors may have meetings with the

38 Rev Rule 87-41

companies they offer their services to, but they are less integral to the company's operations.

4. **Services rendered personally:** Employees offer services personally, rather than passing them off to staff members. Independent contractors, like outside companies, may pass services off to specialists or assistants.
5. **Hiring assistants:** The ability to hire assistants for one's own benefit (without asking for permission from the company) is characteristic of an independent contractor. Like any other outside company, independent contractors make their own hiring (and firing) decisions.
6. **Continuing relationship:** Independent contractors are generally paid by the project. The work ends once the project is done. Employees work on a more continuous basis for the same employer and are paid in regular intervals (by the hour, week, or month).
7. **Set hours of work:** Employees are often required to offer their services at specific times on specific days. Independent contractors often choose when they work.
8. **Full-time required:** Independent contractors cannot offer full-time hours to one company. If they do that, it is difficult (if not impossible) to provide their services to any other firms. In other words, they really can't be independent.
9. **Work done on premises:** If the worker is required to be on the company's premises, they are more likely to be an employee. Independent contractors are more likely to be able to choose where the work is done.
10. **Order of sequence set:** Employees generally must follow a specific sequence or process for how the work is done.

Independent contractors have more freedom to choose the order of how the work is done.

11. **Reports:** Employees are more often required to offer regular reports to the company and their executives.
12. **Payments:** Employees are normally paid at regular intervals (by the hour, week, or month). Independent contractors are generally paid by the project.
13. **Expenses:** Employees are reimbursed for their business expenses. This is not always the case with independent contractors. Unless expense reimbursement is written into a contract, independent contractors must pay their own expenses.
14. **Materials:** Employees generally do not pay for the materials to do a job, but independent contractors do.
15. **Investment:** Independent contractors generally buy their own supplies and equipment to perform the work that they do. This is not the case with employees. Employers usually purchase the equipment that an employee needs to do their work.
16. **Profit or loss:** Since independent contractors generally pay for their own expenses, they may show a profit or loss at the end of the year. This wouldn't be relevant for an employee, as it would be tough for an employee to lose money working at a job!
17. **Multiple employers:** If one is working for multiple companies, they are more like an independent contractor. Employees generally have one or two companies that they work for, not several.
18. **Services offered to the public:** Workers who offer their services openly to the public are more likely to be independent contractors.

19. **Right to fire:** An independent contractor can generally choose who they want to hire and fire. Unless an employee is a manager with this discretion, they cannot do this.
20. **Right to quit:** Employees have the right to quit a job. Most employee contracts are at-will, meaning that an employee can quit whenever they want for nearly any reason (or no reason at all). Independent contractors must complete the jobs and engagements that they are contracted to do.

It should be noted that no single factor is determinative by itself. You should look at all the factors together and the totality of the circumstances to figure out if your workers are employees or independent contractors. Workers do not have a choice in how they are classified. Employers must classify workers based on the nature of their relationship and the twenty factors listed above.[39]

What happens if I misclassify workers?

If an employer treats a worker like an independent contractor when they should be treated as an employee, the employer could be subject to back payroll taxes, IRS and DOL penalties, and interest. They also may need to pay the worker for overtime pay and missed retirement plan contributions. In short, you want to get the classification of workers correct. It can be costly if you don't!

That said, mistakes do happen. If you need to reclassify workers, the IRS offers a way for employers to "come clean" and pay a minimal

39 The DOL rules for classifying workers are similar to the IRS rules in that you must look at the totality of the circumstances to make a determination. However, they are not entirely the same. It is possible to have a worker classified one way for DOL purposes and another for IRS purposes, but this is rare.

amount out of pocket to fix the mistake. This program is called the Voluntary Classification Settlement Program (VCSP). By participating in the VCSP, you agree to prospectively treat the class or classes of workers as employees for future tax periods. The following will then apply:

- You will pay 10% of the employment tax liability that would have been due on compensation paid to the workers for the most recent tax year, determined under the reduced rates of section 3509(a) of the Internal Revenue Code.
- You will not be liable for any interest and penalties on the amount.
- You will not be subject to an employment tax audit with respect to the worker classification of the workers being reclassified under the VCSP for prior years.

In other words, you can fix your mistake going forward, classify workers correctly, and only pay a small amount out of pocket. To participate in the program, you must file Form 8952 and meet specific requirements:

- You must have consistently treated the workers to be reclassified as independent contractors or nonemployees, including filing all required Form 1099s for the previous three years.
- You cannot currently be under an employment tax audit by the IRS or actively under an audit concerning the classification of workers by the DOL or a state government agency.
- If the IRS or the DOL has previously audited you concerning the classification of the workers, you will only be eligible for the program if you have complied with the audit results and are not currently contesting the classification in court.

In short, the VCSP is not for employers who are trying to get around the tax rules. (Presumably, if you are reading this book, you want to do things correctly. So, these situations probably don't apply to you.) It is for employers who have been treating workers as independent contractors by mistake and are looking to come clean.

It should be noted that the VCSP is a federal IRS program. You may still have issues with the DOL or the state taxing authorities (or unemployment office), even if you qualify for the VCSP. However, the program is a good one to know about. Mistakes happen when any business is starting, so knowing how to fix them is imperative.

What's my responsibility for independent contractor taxes?

Yes. If you determine that someone is an independent contractor, you need to keep track of how much you pay them and give them a Form 1099 at the end of the year. A Form 1099 reports how much you paid your contractor for their services during the year. To properly fill out the Form 1099, you need to collect some information from your contractor: their legal name, social security number (or EIN in the case of a company), address, and the type of entity they are (individual, C corporation, S corporation, etc.). If you don't have this information, you won't be able to give your contractor a Form 1099. If you do not provide your contractor with a Form 1099 or if not all the parts are filled out correctly, the IRS will likely charge you a penalty.

The best way to get this information from your contractor is by having them fill out a Form W-9. A Form W-9 is not filed with the IRS. It is filled out by the contractor before they start work for you. You keep it on file and then use the information when it comes time for you to file your Form 1099s at the end of the year. Remember, if you can't complete the Form 1099 correctly, the IRS charges you a penalty, not your contractor. Once they have received payment, there is little incentive for them to fill out the Form W-9 for you. Therefore, you always want to get a Form W-9 upfront before you pay your contractor.

Some payments a business can make do not require a Form 1099. For example, most payments to C corporations do not require a Form 1099. Also, in most instances, you only need to give a Form 1099 to a contractor whom you have paid six hundred dollars or more. Even with these exceptions, though, most companies simply have all companies and contractors they work with fill out a Form 1099. That way, they have the information if they ever need it.

In my experience, some new business owners hesitate to ask their contractors to fill out a Form W-9 because it requires sharing personal information. I always remind them that even very large companies ask for this information from contractors and companies they work with. It is a normal part of business. If someone does not want to fill out a Form W-9, they may be trying to commit tax fraud. Do you really want to be doing business with someone like that? Probably not. Get in the habit of asking for Form W-9s so you can stay in compliance with the IRS.

In addition to tax compliance, you should also have your contractors sign an agreement for the work they are being asked to do. You need to ensure both sides clearly understand the expectations, deadlines, and when payments are due. Also, if the contractor has access to sensitive information, you should have them sign a contract that protects this information and tells them what is permissible (and not permissible) to do with it. Like an employment contract, an independent contractor agreement should cover the entire working relationship. Even if you know the contractor well, you should always have them sign a contract. If things do go sour in the relationship, you want to guarantee you are protected. Not having a contract is never a big deal—until it is!

What if I hire an employee?

If you determine that the worker should be classified as an employee, there are several steps you need to take. First, you need to have them fill out a Form I-9. A Form I-9 verifies that a person is eligible to work in the United States. The due dates for the Form I-9 are as follows:

- Section 1 must be filled out no later than day one of employment.
- Section 2 must be filled out no later than day three of employment. Employee must present authentic documents from the following (see appendix for details on acceptable documents from each list):
- List A (establishes identity and work eligibility) or
- List B (establishes only identity) and
- List C (establishes only employment)

It is important to remember that you do not send the Form I-9 anywhere. You just keep it on file in case you ever need it. Anytime a worker is hired or rehired, you need to have them fill out a Form I-9.[40]

In addition to filling out a Form I-9, employees must complete a Form W-4. A Form W-4 indicates how much federal income tax must be withheld from a person's paycheck each pay period. Like a Form W-9 for a contractor, the Form W-4 also confirms certain information about the taxpayer, including their legal name, address,

40 Technically, you don't have to get a new Form I-9 from a worker in some instances (for example, if they are rehired within a certain length of time). However, it is best practice to always fill out a new form.

and social security number. You should have a new employee fill out the Form W-4 on their first day of employment. All employees are normally subject to federal income tax withholding. The only time a worker would not have any federal income tax withheld is if they had no federal tax liability in the prior year, and they do not expect to have one in the current year either. They would indicate this on the Form W-4 that they fill out.

Like the I-9, the Form W-4 is retained by the employer. Suppose an employee does not fill out a Form W-4 (or fills it out incorrectly). In that case, you need to withhold for that employee using the IRS withholding tables for single taxpayers taking a standard deduction. Also, an employee must always provide you with their social security number.

States that have an income tax usually also have a form like the federal Form W-4 that indicates how much state income tax should be withheld from the employee's paycheck. These forms should also be filled out when the employee first starts. Like contractors, you should also have employees sign an employment contract.

What happens at the end of the year?

At the end of the year, you will give a Form 1099 to all your contractors (normally a Form 1099-NEC) indicating how much you paid them during the year. A copy of the Form 1099 should be sent to each contractor and the IRS. Assuming you only have Form 1099-NECs, these forms must be sent out no later than January 31st. Similarly, you need to give all your employees a copy of their W-2 no later than January 31st. A Form W-2 tells the employee how much they were paid during the year and how much was withheld for federal taxes. Copies of your W-2s will be sent to the Social Security Administration, too.

If you are using a payroll service, it is important to figure out if the payroll service is sending out these forms on your behalf or if you are required to do this under the terms of your contract. Either way, the IRS holds you responsible for completing these tasks. There are significant penalties for not giving employees their W-2s or contractors their 1099s on time!

Copies of W-2s and 1099s are normally sent electronically to the IRS and Social Security Administration respectively along with a transmittal form (a summary sheet) that totals up the number of forms and the dollar amounts on the forms. The transmittal form that gets sent in with your 1099s is a Form 1096. The transmittal form for W-2s is the Form W-3.

Do I need an employee handbook?

When you are first starting a business, you probably don't need an employee handbook. Employee handbooks are used to clarify expectations, commit policies and procedures, and communicate company philosophy. Since most businesses start with only one person (you), this is probably not necessary early on. However, as time goes by and you begin to hire people, you will need an employee handbook.

It is common for employee handbooks to say something about the company's background, mission statement, and philosophy. It clarifies rules and expectations. It will also give an overview of employee benefits, time off, and compensation structure (for example, if and when bonuses will be given), and indicate when employees will become eligible for them. It is common to have employees sign the handbook each year to confirm they have read it and understood what it says.

One common concern from small business owners is whether the employee handbook constitutes an enforceable legal contract. If you refer to the chapter on contracts, five elements need to be present before a document can be considered a valid contract, including consideration. If both sides have not given consideration, then you do not have a contract. Therefore, an employee handbook may or may not be considered a contract depending on whether the five elements are all present or not.

What about terminating employees?

Even under the best employers, people occasionally leave. They leave for new opportunities, changes in their personal lives, or because the situation just wasn't a good fit. Regardless of the reason, it is important to remember to get company property back from the terminated employee and to cut off access to any company files or proprietary information.

Unless the relationship with the employee has been irreparably damaged and there are severe negative feelings, I always like to have exit interviews with employees who are leaving. These can be formal or informal. However, exit interviews allow the employee to give you feedback as an employer. What did you do well? Was there something that you could have done better? As you grow your business and move forward, this can be valuable. Since the employee is leaving, they are likely to be brutally honest! Therefore, this can be an excellent time for you to learn.

I have often found that many employers treat employees who leave with disdain. They have negative feelings because employers feel like they left "their work family." While I believe it is valuable to build camaraderie among your colleagues, having negative feelings towards a departing employee only leads to hurt and may shut the door to future opportunities. It is important to remember that the world is small. If you work long enough in the same industry or location, you are bound to run into the same people. Ask yourself: How many times have you run into someone you worked with in the past out in public? It happens all the time!

Possibly the best career advice I ever received was when I was leaving my first job. I was feeling negatively about how I was treated. A friend and colleague told me it was important for me to "end well." I sucked it up and shook hands with everyone there—people I loved to be around as well as those who made my working life there difficult. I was glad I did. Many of those same people have helped me at various times in building my own business. I have even helped them a time or two. Relationships matter. People matter. To be clear, I am not saying that anyone should ever put up with abuse or harassment at work. That should never be tolerated. However, don't say something when you are walking out the door that you know you will regret later. If you can, try to "end well."

Tips for Getting to Go

1. If you decide to hire someone, consider the type of person you need. What skills must they have? What skills are just nice to have? More experienced employees will likely demand a higher salary. Do you need someone more experienced? Think through these questions before putting together your job description.

2. If an employee is struggling, sometimes the best thing to do is just ask them what is going on. You will be amazed at how much people will tell you if you listen long enough!
3. Hiring and seeing people progress in their careers is one of the greatest joys I have experienced in my professional life. Celebrate when your employees win. Tell them when they have done well. It makes a difference!

EPILOGUE

Calm Down: You Need Patience

"Man, that was awful!" I shook my head in disgust. I was tired, stressed out, and felt like I had just been through an interrogation. In a way, I had been.

"They hated everything. I prepared for weeks, and I thought I had everything covered . . . I guess not. I feel like I failed."

"You didn't." The other voice in the room was much more sedate than my own.

"How in the world are you so chill about this? I mean . . . *terrible*!"

I was now getting fired up at the fact that my boss was not as fired up about the board meeting that just ended as I was. "You were in the same room as I was!" I said in an accusing tone.

"I have one question for you. Did we get the money?" he asked in a confident but monotone voice. His calmness momentarily infuriated me.

"Yes, but . . ." I interjected.

"Stop! When we came into this meeting, our main objective was to get our board to okay giving us more money. That was the goal. The goal was not to get them to like our advertising. We are a startup. There is no way they were going to like our financials. They gave us the money anyway. They must not hate us too bad, Dave. If they did, why would they invest more?"

There are certain times when you can't argue with the logic that is presented to you. After my first board meeting, my boss at the time (now mentor and friend) taught me an important lesson: Startups are hard. Focus on the overall progress and vision of what you are doing. Don't sweat the small stuff. You can't if you are going to continue to move forward.

If you have made it to this part of the book, you may feel overwhelmed. Your excitement over going out on your own may have been partially replaced by feelings of anxiety—the "What the hell did I just do?" feeling. Many an entrepreneur has felt that feeling in the pit of their stomach. I know I felt it that very first day after I quit my job and chose to take a chance on a vision I had for a company. When it is just you and your coffee cup, it can be difficult to face reality.

Here is the truth. No preparation, capital, or knowledge is enough when starting a new business. There is no such thing as a perfect start. There is no such thing as getting it all right. You sometimes feel like you are fumbling along. Take a step back and realize where you have made progress. We tend to focus on the things that are not going well. This is especially true if you are a perfectionist at heart. Try to focus on what is going well and where you have made inroads. As I was reminded when I was a young CFO, sometimes you need to look at the big picture, not perseverate on one piece.

I have told colleagues, journalists, business partners, and anyone else who has asked me about building a small business that there is never enough when you are first starting. There is never enough money. There is never enough time. There is never enough you.

Things never come together fast enough. This is where patience matters. If you keep going and have patience with yourself, things can come together. You need to give it time though, and that can be extremely difficult in the early days.

Whenever I start feeling impatient or stressed about my business, I always do these things. I offer them to you in hopes that they may help when you feel those inevitable frustrations that go along with building something from scratch.

Ask: Do you have more good problems than bad problems?

In business, you always have problems. There are always things you wish you could improve or wish were going more smoothly. The question is whether you have more good problems than bad. Good problems are challenges related to progress or growth. If you feel overwhelmed by the amount of client work you have to do, that may be a good problem. People are interested in your product, and you have almost too much work. Let's be clear: Too much stress can turn negative. Too much client work *is* a problem that you need to solve. However, ultimately, you have customers. Your dream is coming to fruition. Now you need to figure out the next step. Do you hire? Should you start turning away business? What's the right move? In the end, this is a problem you want to have because it means your idea is gaining traction.

Do you have more positive problems than negative ones? If so, you are making progress. Patience and thinking through the issue will help you through it.

Ask: Is your frustration really just passion?

As I discussed in the opening to this book, you must be passionate about what you do to go out on your own. Passion is what gets you by when money is tight. Passion is what gets you by when you put in another long day. Your energy to keep going is fueled by passion. It has to be. Otherwise, you won't be able to keep going once the road becomes rough.

Whenever I feel frustrated, I take a step back and think about the real source of my frustration. Am I just feeling this way because I am so passionate about what I do that I want everything to go right? Is my disappointment, anger, and negative feelings really just a deep desire to make my dream of owning a successful business come true? If it is not, I need to trace back to where my real frustration lies. I also need to figure out if it is something I can alleviate in the present moment. If my feelings are just a manifestation of passion, I need to exercise some patience and remember that things will come together if I give them time.

Ask: Do you still love what you do?

I think this is the most important question to ask yourself when facing adversity with your business. Do you still love what you do? If your frustration undermines your love for the work, then it may be time to hang it up. Try something else. Move on and explore where you can find joy.

If you still love what you do, then whatever adversity you are feeling is a bump in the road. You need to exercise patience and realize that this, too, will pass. You will find a way to keep going. You need to. Your dream is at stake, so you either give up or find a way through it. In reality, giving up is never an option if you really love something. Your heart won't let you stop.

One Last Thought

Starting a business from scratch defies logic. If you look at statistics related to startup businesses, the cold reality is that most startups fail. When you go out on your own, you often give up stability, other opportunities, and even a bit of yourself. However, the fact is that some folks *do* succeed. Businesses do start out of someone's garage. Success does come to some people who bet their last dollar on themselves. It does happen. If you exercise patience when times get tough and focus on the vision of what you want to build, it can happen for you, too!

I sincerely hope this book has helped you see how to get there a bit more clearly. If you have reached go, be brave—and go!

Acknowledgements

There are certain critical points in life's journey. If you don't get the support that you need, you may give up or simply stop trying. I have been lucky enough to have many people pick me up when I have doubted myself and encourage me when I have felt too tired to go on. Thank you to those who have given me the experiences to write about in this book. Without you, I would not have stories and advice to share with others.

I want to thank my mentors, Andrew Rose, Tim MacAleese, and Susan Gaidos. Each of you met me when my career and confidence needed a boost. Thank you for breathing new life into my professional life and encouraging me to go for it all, whether that meant going back to school or running my own business.

I give special thanks to my publicists, Wendy Guarisco and Emilia Gledhill, for helping me find a message to share with the public and reminding me that only I can share my story.

I would also like to express my gratitude to my family for believing in me from the beginning and pushing me to write this book.

Mom and Dad, thanks for listening to me when I was down and celebrating my wins along the way.

To the editorial team at Indigo River Publishing, thank you for championing this work and infusing it with your insightful feedback.

Last, but far from least, my deepest thanks are reserved for my team at Peters Professional Education. I appreciate your tireless efforts to keep the ball rolling as I worked many days and nights on this manuscript. As I have told you all many times, you are the best!

APPENDIX A

Secretaries of State

Alabama: https://www.sos.alabama.gov/

Alaska: https://www.elections.alaska.gov/

Arizona: https://azsos.gov/

Arkansas: https://www.sos.arkansas.gov/

California: https://www.sos.ca.gov/

Colorado: https://www.sos.state.co.us/

Connecticut: https://portal.ct.gov/SOTS

Delaware: https://sos.delaware.gov/

Florida: https://dos.myflorida.com/elections/

Georgia: https://sos.ga.gov/

Hawaii: https://elections.hawaii.gov/

Idaho: https://sos.idaho.gov/

Illinois: https://www.cyberdriveillinois.com/

Indiana: https://www.in.gov/sos/

Iowa: https://sos.iowa.gov/

Kansas: https://sos.kansas.gov/

Kentucky: https://sos.ky.gov/

Louisiana: https://www.sos.la.gov/

Maine: https://www.maine.gov/sos/

Maryland: https://elections.maryland.gov/

Massachusetts: https://www.sec.state.ma.us/

Michigan: https://www.michigan.gov/sos/

Minnesota: https://www.sos.state.mn.us/

Mississippi: https://www.sos.ms.gov/

Missouri: https://s1.sos.mo.gov/

Montana: https://sosmt.gov/

Nebraska: https://sos.nebraska.gov/

Nevada: https://www.nvsos.gov/

New Hampshire: https://sos.nh.gov/

New Jersey: https://www.state.nj.us/state/

New Mexico: https://www.sos.nm.gov/

New York: https://www.dos.ny.gov/

North Carolina: https://www.sosnc.gov/

North Dakota: https://sos.nd.gov/

Ohio: https://www.ohiosos.gov/

Oklahoma: https://sos.ok.gov/

Oregon: https://sos.oregon.gov/

Pennsylvania: https://www.pennsylvaniasos.gov/

Rhode Island: https://sos.ri.gov/

South Carolina: https://sos.sc.gov/

South Dakota: https://sdsos.gov/

Tennessee: https://sos.tn.gov/

Texas: https://www.sos.state.tx.us/

Utah: https://elections.utah.gov/

Vermont: https://sos.vermont.gov/

Virginia: https://www.commonwealth.virginia.gov/

Washington: https://www.sos.wa.gov/

West Virginia: https://sos.wv.gov/

Wisconsin: https://sos.wi.gov/

Wyoming: https://sos.wyo.gov/

APPENDIX B

State Departments of Taxation

Alabama: https://revenue.alabama.gov/

Alaska: https://tax.alaska.gov/

Arizona: https://azdor.gov/

Arkansas: https://www.dfa.arkansas.gov/

California: https://www.cdtfa.ca.gov/

Colorado: https://tax.colorado.gov/

Connecticut: https://portal.ct.gov/DRS

Delaware: https://revenue.delaware.gov/

Florida: https://floridarevenue.com/

Georgia: https://dor.georgia.gov/

Hawaii: https://tax.hawaii.gov/

Idaho: https://tax.idaho.gov/

Illinois: https://www2.illinois.gov/rev/Pages/default.aspx

Indiana: https://www.in.gov/dor/

Iowa: https://tax.iowa.gov/

Kansas: https://www.ksrevenue.org/

Kentucky: https://revenue.ky.gov/

Louisiana: https://revenue.louisiana.gov/

Maine: https://www.maine.gov/revenue/

Maryland: https://www.marylandtaxes.gov/

Massachusetts: https://www.mass.gov/orgs/massachusetts-department-of-revenue

Michigan: https://www.michigan.gov/taxes/

Minnesota: https://www.revenue.state.mn.us/

Mississippi: https://www.dor.ms.gov/

Missouri: https://dor.mo.gov/

Montana: https://mtrevenue.gov/

Nebraska: https://revenue.nebraska.gov/

Nevada: https://tax.nv.gov/

New Hampshire: https://www.revenue.nh.gov/

New Jersey: https://www.state.nj.us/treasury/taxation/

New Mexico: https://www.tax.newmexico.gov/

New York: https://www.tax.ny.gov/

North Carolina: https://www.ncdor.gov/

North Dakota: https://www.nd.gov/tax/

Ohio: https://tax.ohio.gov/

Oklahoma: https://www.oklahoma.gov/tax.html

Oregon: https://www.oregon.gov/dor/

Pennsylvania: https://www.revenue.pa.gov/

Rhode Island: https://tax.ri.gov/

South Carolina: https://dor.sc.gov/

South Dakota: https://dor.sd.gov/

Tennessee: https://www.tn.gov/revenue.html

Texas: https://comptroller.texas.gov/taxes/

Utah: https://tax.utah.gov/

Vermont: https://tax.vermont.gov/

Virginia: https://www.tax.virginia.gov/

Washington: https://dor.wa.gov/

West Virginia: https://tax.wv.gov/

Wisconsin: https://www.revenue.wi.gov/

Wyoming: https://www.wyomingbusiness.org/tax/

APPENDIX C

Acceptable Documents for Form I-9 verification

LIST A **Documents that Establish Both Identity and Employment Authorization**	OR	LIST B **Documents that Establish Identity**	AND	LIST C **Documents that Establish Employment Authorization**
1. U.S. Passport or U.S. Passport Card		**1.** Driver's license or ID card issued by a State or outlying possession of the United States provided it contains a photograph or information such as name, date of birth, gender, height, eye color, and address		**1.** A Social Security Account Number card, unless the card includes one of the following restrictions: **(1)** NOT VALID FOR EMPLOYMENT **(2)** VALID FOR WORK ONLY WITH INS AUTHORIZATION **(3)** VALID FOR WORK ONLY WITH DHS AUTHORIZATION
2. Permanent Resident Card or Alien Registration Receipt Card (Form I-551)		**2.** ID card issued by federal, state or local government agencies or entities, provided it contains a photograph or information such as name, date of birth, gender, height, eye color, and address		**2.** Certification of report of birth issued by the Department of State (Forms DS-1350, FS-545, FS-240)
3. Foreign passport that contains a temporary I-551 stamp or temporary I-551 printed notation on a machine-readable immigrant visa		**3.** School ID card with a photograph		**3.** Original or certified copy of birth certificate issued by a State, county, municipal authority, or territory of the United States bearing an official seal
4. Employment Authorization Document that contains a photograph (Form I-766)		**4.** Voter's registration card		**4.** Native American tribal document
5. For an individual temporarily authorized to work for a specific employer because of his or her status or parole: **a.** Foreign passport; and **b.** Form I-94 or Form I-94A that has the following: **(1)** The same name as the passport; and **(2)** An endorsement of the individual's status or parole as long as that period of endorsement has not yet expired and the proposed employment is not in conflict with any restrictions or limitations identified on the form.		**5.** U.S. Military card or draft record **6.** Military dependent's ID card **7.** U.S. Coast Guard Merchant Mariner Card **8.** Native American tribal document **9.** Driver's license issued by a Canadian government authority		**5.** U.S. Citizen ID Card (Form I-197) **6.** Identification Card for Use of Resident Citizen in the United States (Form I-179)
6. Passport from the Federated States of Micronesia (FSM) or the Republic of the Marshall Islands (RMI) with Form I-94 or Form I-94A indicating nonimmigrant admission under the Compact of Free Association Between the United States and the FSM or RMI		**For persons under age 18 who are unable to present a document listed above:** **10.** School record or report card **11.** Clinic, doctor, or hospital record **12.** Day-care or nursery school record		**7.** Employment authorization document issued by the Department of Homeland Security For examples, see **Section 7** and **Section 13** of the M-274 on **uscis.gov/i-9-central**. The Form I-766, Employment Authorization Document, is a List A, **Item Number 4.** document, not a List C document.

www.ingramcontent.com/pod-product-compliance
Lightning Source LLC
LaVergne TN
LVHW020719110826
845149LV00012B/2330

* 9 7 8 1 9 6 9 9 3 5 1 8 3 *